Proverbs 3:5&6

The Distilled Essence of the Christian Life

Bob Beasley

Living Stone Books

About the Author

Bob Beasley is a native of Nashville, Tennessee, but lived most of his life in San Diego, California. He now lives with his wife, Amy, in Hartville, Ohio. Bob is a graduate of Westminster Theological Seminary in California and has three daughters and seven grandchildren. In addition to his writing ministry, Bob teaches seminary classes in Ukraine. He is the author of *The Wisdom of Proverbs*, *Loving King Jesus: The Joyous Freedom of Obedience*, *101 Portraits of Jesus in the Hebrew Scriptures*, and with Amy, *Wisdom for Women*. He has also paraphrased into modern English the 1737 William Whiston translation of Flavius Josephus's first century *The Jewish Wars* and *The Life of Flavius Josephus*.

This book is dedicated to the glory of
the Creator and Sustainer of all life,
the Lord Jesus Christ.

PROVERBS 3:5&6: The Distilled Essence of the Christian Life

Unless otherwise indicated, all Scripture quotations are from the Holy Bible, English Standard Version © (ESV ©), copyright © 2001 by Crossway, a publishing ministry of Good News Publishers. Used by permission. All rights reserved.

Scripture quotations marked (KJV) are from The Holy Bible, King James Version.

ISBN: 978-0-9890922-4-1

Copyright: 2016 by Living Stone Books

Edited by Nat Belz

Cover Artwork: www.ebooklaunch.com

Printed in the United States of America. All Rights Reserved.
Under international Copyright Law, no part of this publication may be reproduced, stored, or transmitted by any means—electronic, mechanical, photogenic (photocopy), recording, or otherwise—without written permission from the author.

Table of Contents

Foreword 7

Chapter 1: "Trust In The Lord With All Your Heart" 11

Chapter 2: "And Do Not Lean On Your Own Understanding" 52

Chapter 3: "In All Your Ways Acknowledge Him" 92

Chapter 4: "And He Will Make Straight Your Paths" 138

Afterword... 165

Abbreviated Bibliography:.. 167

Appendix: Verses on Man and Depravity..................................... 169

Acknowledgments

I want to thank the many friends who have helped and encouraged me in the long process of completing this small volume. In no particular order, these men and women have been particularly insightful: Nat and Mindy Belz, Allyson and Mark van den Herik, Stephen and Theresa Todd, Merle and Donna Messer, Dale and Susan Slusser, Jim and Susan Phillis, Dick and Marta Bowser, and Denton and Jean White. Any errors or typos that you may find are mine alone. My special thanks and love go out to my wife, Amy, who helped immensely with editing, and who puts up with the many hours I sit at my computer, hunting and pecking out books.

Proverbs 3:5&6

The Distilled Essence of the Christian Life

Foreword

*"Trust in the LORD with all your heart,
and do not lean on your own understanding.
In all your ways acknowledge him,
and he will make straight your paths."*

From my earliest memories, my father claimed these simple verses as two of his favorites in God's Word. They were his "life verses," as we might say today. I know that many of you also claim them as your life verses. But it was to be many years before Christ kick-started my sinful heart and led me to follow Him in faith that I was enabled to see the wisdom contained in them. A mere 29 words in Solomon's proverbs, yet in them is found the summary instruction for the life and practice of every one who desires to truly emulate Christ. Now I, too, claim them as my favorites in the Bible—my life verses. I hope that as you read, if you haven't already done so, they will also be your favorites.

By God's grace, I received Christ and was baptized at the age of 9 during Vacation Bible School at Immanuel Baptist Church in Nashville, Tennessee. But even though I grew up in a Christian home, I was Christian in name only for many years. I thought Christ was my Savior, but He was not my Lord. It wasn't until I was 33, and married with three daughters, that Christ's Spirit resurrected me to true faith and obedience. At that time my "understanding" had been fully united to the ways of the world, the flesh, and the devil. They were the true "lords" of my heart. But when Christ's Spirit took command of my mind and soul in 1971, He brought me to a distinctly opposite way of thinking. He claimed rightly to be my only Authority and Master and sought to *"restore my soul [and] lead me in paths of righteousness for his name's sake"* (Psalm 23:3).

It hasn't been an easy task. Having lived most of my life in San Diego, I am familiar with the Navy. I use the metaphor of a Navy captain seeking to turn a battleship around 180 degrees at full speed. It isn't done on a dime. Likewise, it has taken a long time to turn Beasley's ship around, and Jesus has much work ahead before I go home to be with Him. But these short 29 words have helped me immensely, by attuning my mind to the necessity of walking by faith and not by sight (2 Corinthians 5:7).

Our Lord Jesus is real. He is the Preexistent One—the Creator of all that exists. He is not only all-powerful, He also has the will to rule this world and is sovereign in every minute aspect of its history. *"He upholds the universe by the word of his power"* (Hebrews 1:3). His written Word—the Bible in both Old and New Testaments—is alive and powerful and true. It is sufficient for our life and practice as His followers.

Are you like me? Why is it so difficult for us to grab hold of these facts and acknowledge Him for who He truly is? To give Jesus full credit and the submission He deserves as sovereign Lord? To follow Him wholeheartedly? It is because the old sin nature seeks to drag us back into unbelief and sin. We want to lean on our own understanding. We want to usurp the credit and glory only He deserves and acknowledge ourselves or some other idol as "lord." We want to direct our own paths. In doing so, we are our own worst enemies.

C. S. Lewis wrote these familiar words: "We are half-hearted creatures, fooling about with drink and sex and ambition when infinite joy is offered us, like an ignorant child who wants to go on making mud pies in a slum because he cannot imagine what is meant by the offer of a holiday at the sea. We are far too easily pleased" (*The Weight of Glory* - 1949).

Dr. Lewis had me in mind when he wrote that. Maybe you too? We trust Christ—our loving God—for salvation. He is our ultimate hope as the Conquerer of death. Why can't we trust Him for an abundantly joyful life in the here and now? We certainly can. He provides the will, the power, and the way. His paths are far better than ours. His ways and power are so much superior to ours. And the distilled essence of following Him joyously is set forth in these few words of Proverbs 3:5&6.

One final thing. I have touched on many subjects too large to deal with in this book. I hope the reader will take an interest in the subjects discussed and study further using books listed in the bibliography.

Some time ago, Amy, and I attended a conference in Dallas, Texas, and had dinner one night with a friend who is a professor at a Christian college. I mentioned that I was writing a book on Proverbs 3:5&6 and he responded, "That's my life verse!" Why is that true for so many Christians? This little volume seeks to answer that question. May God bless you richly as you grow to bring honor and glory to our great God and Savior, Jesus Christ, trusting Him with all of your heart, leaning not on your own understanding, acknowledging Him in all your ways, and walking on the solid and straight path of His righteousness. That's the distilled essence of our lives in Christ.

Bob Beasley

Hartville, Ohio

Chapter I

"Trust in the LORD With All of Your Heart…"

WHAT DOES IT MEAN TO "TRUST" IN THE LORD? Jesus commanded us in John 14:1, *"Let not your hearts be troubled. Believe in God; believe also in me."* What did He mean by the word, *"believe"*? I suppose most of us know the answer, at least partially. He meant to cast the full weight of one's cares and fears upon God and Himself. He meant to rely upon, or have confidence in, the ability of God to accomplish what He has said He would accomplish. "Believe" meant to trust, and trust is an assured expectation that a promise will be kept.

This afternoon, I need to get in my car and drive to the supermarket for groceries. I am confident that the car will get me there and back without breaking down. Why? Because I have put on 125,678 miles over the past 10 years and my auto has hardly caused me one bit of trouble. I have maintained it properly and recently purchased a new battery and new tires, and filled the tank with gasoline. I have confidence—trust—in my automobile's promise to start quickly and bring me back safely. Ah, but there's a problem. My car cannot really promise to do that, because lurking out there in my town are other cars. I can neither trust them fully, nor their drivers. My experience has taught me, (through a few crumpled fenders over the years), that I need to be very cautious out there on the highway. Of course, I have to have some trust—faith—in other vehicles and their drivers, or I wouldn't get out on the road, but my faith in them is limited by how trustworthy they really are. So it is with trusting God. Can we really know enough about the God of the Bible to truly and completely trust Him?

One reason that we don't trust God perfectly—with all of our hearts—is because we do not know Him as well as we should. Trust involves knowledge. I have a successful history of operating my vehicle—a gracious gift of God—and therefore I trust it to get to the supermarket and back without a mechanical problem. But I don't have sufficient historical knowledge of other vehicles and their drivers' capabilities, so I can't trust them—or myself!—fully. How can we expect to trust God fully—with all of our hearts—if we don't really know the God in whom we trust? That's the subject of Chapter 3, *"In all your ways acknowledge Him…"* For now, let's look at what our verses say about the office or title of the God in whom we are to trust.

"Yahweh," the Great "I AM" of the Burning Bush

The Hebrew word for "LORD" here is Yahweh. (Notice that "LORD" is spelled in all capital letters. The Hebrew "Lord" using lower case letters means Adonai, or "master" or "owner.") The original Hebrew has no vowels, but if they are added, the name for God here, YHWH, becomes Yahweh, or as we sometimes say in English, "Jehovah." (You may also see this name of God referred to as "the Tetragrammaton," which is just a sixty-dollar word that means "four letters.") The name Yahweh means "He who is," or "I am that I am." Remember when Moses heard the voice from the burning bush in Exodus 3? The voice revealed Himself to be Yahweh.

In announcing His name, Yahweh," God was proclaiming several things about Himself. First, by this title, He claimed to be the God who exists, who actually *is*. Throughout the Old Testament we run into lots of phony "gods" and "goddesses" like Baal, Dagon, Ashtoreth, and so forth. But they don't really exist, except in the minds of those who bowed down to them. Dr. R.C. Sproul likes to say that such idols are merely "Fig Newtons" of someone's imagination. (This is not to say that Satan and the demonic spirits aren't real.) Jehovah is the only true God, and the only supreme being who actually exists, and who communicates His existence and character to us, His creatures, through His creation, His Word, and His earthly ministry.

Second, God says to us by His revealed name, Yahweh, that since He is the only God who exists, He is the preexistent Creator of the universe. He has always existed. To understand our world and universe without a Creator is to deny all reason, which many do today. Why is there something rather than nothing? Look no further than your hand, an amazing instrument. Did it come into existence by mere "chance?" No. It was designed by the preexistent Yahweh—the "I Am" God who has always existed.

A conversation is recorded for us between Jesus and the Pharisees in John 8:48-58. Jesus makes the amazing statement,

> "'Your father Abraham rejoiced that he would see my day. He saw it and was glad.' So the Jews said to him, 'You are not yet fifty years old, and have you seen Abraham?' Jesus said to them, 'Truly, truly, I say to you, before Abraham was, I am.' So they picked up stones to throw at him, but Jesus hid himself and went out of the temple" (vv 56-58).

In stating He was older than Abraham, Jesus claimed eternal existence. Notice that in Jesus's use of the words "*I am,*" the Pharisees knew exactly who He was claiming to be. This is why the Pharisees and teachers of the law plotted to take His life. They considered His statements blasphemous. (For a fascinating study, look up all of Jesus's many "*I Am*" statements in John's gospel.) But the Apostle Paul speaks the truth about Jesus in Colossians 1:15-17:

> "He is the image of the invisible God, the firstborn of all creation. For by him all things were created, in heaven and on earth, visible and invisible, whether thrones or dominions or rulers or authorities—all things were created through him and for him. And he is before all things, and in him all things hold together."

Third, since Yahweh—Jesus—created the universe, He owns it. He is Lord of it. That is to say, He's the ultimate Boss or Authority. Jesus is the Lord God, Creator of heaven and earth, to whom all authority in heaven and on earth has been given (Matthew 28:18). Jesus is He who "*upholds the universe by the word of his power*" (Hebrews 1:3), providentially watching over and caring for His creation. That's what "Yahweh" means. The word "LORD" and the Old Testament Hebrew word "Yahweh" always point us to the Lord Jesus.

Deism, the Enlightenment, and Materialism

In a real sense, many Christians today have reverted to "deism," a false view of God popular in the 18th century. Several of our founding fathers in America (such as Thomas Jefferson) were deists. They believed in a Creator God, but thought that God had now sort of lost interest in His creation, and had kicked back watching how events on earth would unfold. A deist views God as a sort of clockmaker who wound up his new clock, and now is just watching it keep time. But the Bible assures us that the true God—Yahweh—who created the heavens and the earth, is now managing every minute detail of His creation for His glory, and for his children's great and eternal benefit. No maverick electron exists that is outside of God's control. If electrons (or quarks)—the tiniest elements in creation—aren't controlled by our all-powerful God, He controls nothing! We call God's control His "sovereignty." He not only has the infinite power to rule all events, God has the sovereign *will* to rule as well.

In the so-called Enlightenment period of world history back in the 18th century, many began to throw away belief in the supernatural. Instead, philosophers began to see the world in merely materialistic or naturalistic terms. This means that they believed the universe could be explained through natural reason—or natural causes—and so God was no longer needed. For the materialist, if you can't see it, taste it, touch it, smell it, or hear it—it doesn't exist. So much for the invisible God! This view was later enhanced by the work of a naturalist named Charles Darwin. Eighteenth century philosophers such as Immanuel Kant and David Hume championed such materialism, which has had a profound effect on Western worldviews even to this day. But, interestingly, Immanuel Kant reasoned that the idea of a God was necessary in order for society to prosper. Men and women needed to fear that they would be ultimately caught and punished for committing acts that were harmful to the social order.

The God of Kant's reasoning needed to be, first of all, a God who was holy and just. If this God was merely like us, He might not care very much about people's misbehavior, and therefore about justice. So Kant's imagined God needed to be a God of righteous holiness and justice. Secondly, for Kant, this God needed to be able to know all things perfectly—to be omniscient. Otherwise, how could he know the activities of all the people in the world, much less understand their motives? Thirdly, this God had to be omnipotent. He had to possess the infinite power to carry out His justice, and to bring about ultimate punishment. The God Kant described is the God of the Bible. What Kant didn't understand was that this God is also the God of grace who offers a way out of judgment through simple, child-like faith in Jesus. We now turn to a crucial first step in trusting God—trusting Him and Him alone for salvation.

Trusting God for Salvation

Back in the 1990s a rather frivolous Christian discussion took place which was called the "Lordship" debate. It began with some well-meaning theologians proposing that to be saved, one needed only to trust Jesus as Savior but not necessarily as Lord. The notion divided the true Jesus into two parts—Savior on the one hand and Lord on the other.

But Christ's Godhood is total. He can't be divided. He is the Lord God, the second person of the Trinity. He is both Savior and Lord, without division or mixture, and we need to receive Him as both Lord and Savior in order to be assured of our salvation. To call Jesus Savior and not Lord, like I did in the early years of my life, is like calling oneself a pianist yet never touching a keyboard. It's like calling oneself the starting quarterback, yet never throwing a football. The cause of the "Lordship" debate, in my mind at least, was due to a gross misunderstanding of the Gospel and of the Great Commission.

In the Great Commission of Matthew 28:19-20, Jesus commanded His Church,

> *"All authority in heaven and on earth has been given to me. Go therefore and make disciples of all nations, baptizing them in the name of the Father and of the Son and of the Holy Spirit, teaching them to observe all that I have commanded you. And behold, I am with you always, to the end of the age."*

These are the words of the Lord God, who is in view in Proverbs 3:5 as "the LORD—Yahweh." This is the God whom we are to trust.

"Trust God for what? What can we trust the Lord God to do?" If you have never trusted Christ, let me begin by saying that the first thing we trust the Lord Jesus to do is to save us. "Save us from what?" We need Him to save us from His own eternal wrath. Later in this chapter, and in Chapter 2, we discuss what the Bible has to say about the human heart. For now, let me just say that the Bible says we humans in our natural state are ungodly sinners, dead in our trespasses and sins and enemies of God. To sin is to be in cosmic rebellion against God and His law.

For instance, Colossians 1:21 speaks of us in this way; *"And you, who once were alienated and hostile in mind, doing evil deeds. . ."* The consequence of such a state is revealed by Jesus in Matthew 23:33 speaking to the Pharisees (and to all us sinners), *"You serpents, you brood of vipers, how are you to escape being sentenced to hell?"* But Paul goes on to say in Colossians 1:22 that, *"[Christ] has now reconciled in his body of flesh by his death, in order to present you holy and blameless and above reproach before him..."*

How is this possible? This same LORD whom we are to trust in Proverbs 3:5&6, came to this earth as a man, born of a virgin without the taint of sin, lived a life of perfect obedience to God, which our first father Adam had failed to do. The God-man, Jesus, then died a sacrificial death on the Cross of Calvary to pay for both the penalty and the guilt of His people's sin, and rose again for our justification—to make us *"...holy in his sight, without blemish and free from accusation"* (Colossians 1:22). By His grace God then gives the new believer the faith that is the evidence of the renewal that has begun to take place in his sinful, unbelieving heart (Hebrews 11:1). We trust Christ and Christ alone for our salvation, for as Ephesians 2:8-9 says, *"For by grace you have been saved through faith. And this is not your own doing; it is the gift of God, not a result of works, so that no one may boast."* We'll talk more about our "works" in Chapter 2, but let's now look at other areas where many of us Christians fail to trust in the LORD with all of our heart.

As I mentioned in the foreword, I had been raised in a Christian home and had all the advantages of listening to God's Word preached for many years. Plus, I had the examples of my godly parents. But my heart was so far removed from God that I wanted nothing to do with Him. I had my own hopes, my own ambitions, my own plans, and they had nothing to do with a holy God. I wanted to have fun and Christianity didn't look like a way of accomplishing the fun I had in mind. I believed for years that Christians were all scrambling over one another trying to outdo each other in pleasing this mysterious, holy God. They were trying somehow to work their way into His heaven. I knew I was a sinner and had no chance of making that trip. Therefore I wouldn't even get into the race.

And then that day arrived in 1971 when the Holy Spirit opened my spiritual eyes and sinful heart and I understood that salvation is purely and completely God's work, and not anything I could possibly do for myself. Even though God's Spirit had begun a good work in me some twenty-four years before, I had never truly responded in faith and obedience. I finally understood that I was indeed a sinner and the only solution to my sin problem was to trust Christ alone. The wonderful hymn goes, "Jesus paid it all, all to Him I owe. Sin had left its crimson stain, He washed it white as snow." If you have never trusted God for salvation, I urge you to do that now. We are saved from God's eternal wrath not by the worthless "good works" that we do, but by the effective promise of salvation through trusting in Christ alone, through what Jesus accomplished through His life, death, and resurrection. (See Chapter 2 for more on "good works.")

Scriptural Examples of Men and Women who Trusted God

We don't have to look far in either the Old Testament or the New Testament to see examples of men and women who either trusted God with every part of their lives—wholeheartedly—or who didn't trust Him at all. Many, in fact, trusted God with a portion of their heart, but leaned heavily on their own understanding. Let's look at some examples of those who trusted God completely. Later, we'll look at other examples of men and women who did not fully trust in God.

Noah and the Great Flood

We're told in Hebrews 11:7, *"By faith Noah, being warned by God concerning events as yet unseen, in reverent fear constructed an ark for the saving of his household. By this he condemned the world and became an heir of the righteousness that comes by faith."* It had never rained upon the earth when Noah began to construct an enormous ship (Genesis 2:5-6). Instead, a mist came up from the ground to water the soil. There may not even have been an ocean to float it in! But God told Noah to build this gigantic craft that was 75 feet wide, 400 feet long, and 45 feet high. Can you imagine? That's the size of giant ocean liners and commercial ships of our day! It took Noah one hundred years to build it. I have always wanted to build a small sailboat, but don't have the nerve to start the project. I cannot even imagine building a huge ark. All the while, can you imagine how those who passed by must have scoffed at Noah's work? He was the laughing stock of the world before the flood. Noah risked his reputation—everything—on the promise of God.

All the while he was building, Noah took time to try to explain to those who ridiculed him about the coming flood. He preached to them. God was going to open up the skies to rain down the waters in the heavens above. God was going to release the fountains in the ground beneath their feet. An incredible catastrophe was coming. One could be saved only by faith, a faith proven by entering the huge ark. He preached this message for 100 years. And of the thousands upon thousands who must have heard the message, not one person believed him. (People lived a lot longer in those days. As the great flood came upon the earth, it has been estimated that millions of people died in it.) Oh, they ultimately believed, but by that time they were in water over their heads, and perishing in the flood. The ark is an Old Testament picture of Christ. Men and women today are trapped in willing unbelief, even though the proclamation of the truth of our ark—the Lord Jesus—is present in personal evangelism, books, pulpits, on radio and television, and on the Internet. Noah and his family were saved by faith—faith that what God had promised to do He would do. By God's grace alone, Noah trusted God wholeheartedly through persecution and isolation, and God saved both him and his family. (See Genesis 6:9 through 9:18 for Noah's whole story.) Noah's story is a wonderful picture of what it looks like to trust fully in God, not just in a momentary way, but over long years of hardship and suffering.

Abraham the Moon Worshiper

Abraham is the spiritual father of those who are saved by faith alone in God. Probably a wealthy man, he lived in the city of Ur of the Chaldees. Once a coastal city near the mouth of the Euphrates on the Persian Gulf, Ur is now well inland, somewhat south of the Euphrates on its right bank. The city's patron deity was Nanna, the Sumerian moon god. The name of the city is derived from the god's name—URIM—the Sumerian form of Nanna. So Abraham was from a city where the moon god was worshiped. Like you and me, Abraham, then called "Abram," was an idolater (see the discussion of idolatry in Chapter 2). Then, one day,

"Now the LORD said to Abram, 'Go from your country and your kindred and your father's house to the land that I will show you. And I will make of you a great nation, and I will bless you and make your name great, so that you will be a blessing. I will bless those who bless you, and him who dishonors you I will curse, and in you all the families of the earth shall be blessed'"
(Genesis 12:1-3).

Abram, a well-heeled man living in a nice city by the sea, was probably respected by all who knew him. He was about to leave all that behind. Can you imagine what Abram's wife Sarai said to him? "Where are we going, honey?" she must have asked.

"I have no idea," Abram must have said. "But I trust in the One who has called me. Here we are in Ur. We have everything we need but children, and my name means 'father.' It's very embarrassing. But God has promised to make me into a great nation—to be a blessing to all nations. That means children! So, wherever He leads us we will follow."

Can you imagine what Sarai must have thought? Abram must have been talking about the God with whom he had begun to trust, but still, I'm certain it wasn't an easy thing for her to just pack up her things and hit the road. Nevertheless, that's what she did. Sarai must have replied, "OK husband, I hope you know what you're doing!" She believed her husband was trustworthy, and so she followed him.

Abram had to believe that the One who called Him was trustworthy. He had faith that Yahweh would neither fail him nor disappoint him. Did Abram really know for certain—without a doubt—that God could be trusted? No. I'm sure he had his doubts. But he set out on a journey to an unknown place, traveling merely on the promises of the One who called him out of his home in Ur of the Chaldees. He was walking not by sight, but by faith. He was risking everything in order to allow Yahweh to prove He is trustworthy. That's what you and I are to do also. We are to risk all for God. We step out in faith, trusting God, and God always proves Himself trustworthy.

We might ask ourselves if Abram ultimately found God trustworthy. According to his earliest expectations, maybe not. Abram probably thought, "I'm going to be great! I'll be a great nation!" His walk to an unknown land had many surprises and seeming setbacks. Many, many years passed before the blessing of fatherhood came to be in his son, Isaac. God's promise of a son for the wandering couple ultimately became a reality. In the interim, God had changed Abram's name to "Abraham," which meant something like "father of many." Can you imagine the jokes and laughter behind his back? He also had trouble along the way with wars with several kings and trouble with his nephew, Lot. His herdsmen quarreled with others over water rights. Pharaoh tried to take Sarai into his harem. There was trouble and conflict at every turn.

One day, God told Abraham *"Take your son, your only son Isaac, whom you love, and go to the land of Moriah, and offer him there as a burnt offering on one of the mountains of which I shall tell you"* (Genesis 22:2). What! Kill the child of promise? But Abraham trusted God and did what God told him to do, even though killing Isaac was directly opposite to God's promise of making Abraham's descendants into a great nation. Ultimately, God Himself provided the sacrifice in a ram caught in a thicket. Abraham's faith was tested in a mighty way. But he reasoned that even if he had to kill his one and only son, God could raise Isaac from the dead (Hebrews 11:19). Ultimately, God would provide another sacrifice on that same mountain. This time, God's Son, Jesus, would die as a sacrificial offering for the sins of His people. Abraham walked by faith and found a trustworthy God. But there were times when Abraham's trust in Yahweh waned. He hid in other kingdoms, fearing for his life. He told lies. He had a child, Ishmael, by Sarah's servant, Hagar. Rather than trusting God, he took the matter of an heir into his own hands. Ultimately, Abraham only owned one little piece of real estate—a cave where he buried Sarah. It perhaps didn't turn out like he first expected.

But we must ask ourselves, was Abraham disappointed in God's promises? Not at all. We're told in Hebrews 11:10, *"For [Abraham] was looking forward to the city that has foundations, whose designer and builder is God."* Abraham came to understand that the blessings God had promised him were not just for himself and Sarah, but for many others—for millions of people like you and me. He had his earthly eyes on heavenly things, not earthly things that are here today and gone tomorrow. In the same way, God has blessed and continues to bless unseen others by those who walk by faith in Him alone. We, too, may need our expectations transformed.

Joseph and His Ornery Brothers

The story of Joseph and his brothers is one of the most familiar stories in the Bible. It's about a young man whose brothers tied him up and sold him into slavery. Judah and the rest of Joseph's brothers were going to kill him and probably thought selling him instead to a passing caravan was a kindness! Can you imagine such a thing? What would you think if you were in Joseph's shoes? There you are in a foreign country where you don't speak the language and you have no friends. You're standing on the slave market steps as everybody investigates the condition of your teeth and stares at your naked body. Then, you are sold as a slave to a guy named Potiphar, where you run into all sorts of trouble in his home. You refuse to have an affair with Potiphar's wife (which might have been a profitable thing to do in the mind of a pagan). But because of your trust in God, you refuse her advances. Instead of being thanked by Potiphar, you are falsely accused and thrown into jail to languish for years.

Ultimately, Joseph is released from prison and elevated to the second in command in all of Egypt. What was Joseph's "secret" that allowed him to survive and prosper through trouble and suffering? It was simply this: Through thick and thin, through false accusations and malice, Joseph trusted the LORD with all of his heart, and leaned not on his own understanding. Joseph trusted that the goodness, grace, and sovereignty of the LORD would see him through any circumstance. And he was right! We'll speak more about this ancient patriarch later.

Rahab the Prostitute and the Hebrew Spies

Joshua 2:1-24 tells the story of the faith of this woman, a prostitute in the city of Jericho. Jericho was a fortified city, a military outpost—a mighty fortress—impregnable in that day. Do you remember the old hit song, "You and Me Against the World"? Rahab, by faith, stood up against her world, all by herself. But Yahweh supported her. Moses died in the wilderness and had turned his leadership of the children of Israel over to Joshua, whom God ordered to enter the Promised Land across the river Jordan. Standing in his way was this city of Jericho. He sent two trusted men into the city to spy on it—for one thing to get information, and for the other to save Rahab, (even though they probably didn't know that when they set out.)

How do we know that God intended to save Rahab? Remember that God was directing the Hebrew spies. Did God know about Rahab? Of course. Did He know of her faith? Yes. Did Yahweh direct the spies exactly where to go? Yes. They had no immoral purposes as some have wrongfully said. They went specifically to her establishment. They knew precisely where to go! They were on a secret mission for Yahweh. Rahab may have been forced to succumb to prostitution just to support her household. The Bible does not say. But that's the way she survived in pagan Jericho. Isn't it also interesting that the very first story in the Promised Land is about a woman, and a prostitute at that? In the Bible, God's mercy is always revealed before his wrath.

Rahab's had three strikes against her. First, she's a Gentile. Like the Moabitess Ruth, she is outside the Hebrew community of faith. Second, she's an Amorite, among the worst of the Gentile nations facing Joshua. The Amorites sacrificed their children to their gods. Third, and finally, she's a prostitute. Some try to soft-soap her profession, but Rahab reminds us that God only saves sinners. Rahab was no worse than any of us. We all have prostituted ourselves before a holy God in one way or another by following false gods of our own making. (See Chapter 2 on Idolatry.)

Rahab had one BIG thing going for her—she knew about Yahweh. She had heard and she had believed in Him. As Romans 10:17 says: *"So faith comes from hearing, and hearing through the word of Christ."* God had spoken to her heart through her ears and her mind. How? Probably through the men coming from the far countries to her establishment. "Have you heard what happened in Egypt?" someone may have asked. A traveler probably told her about the miraculous crossing of the Red Sea.

Did Rahab know a lot about God? Probably not. It's likely she had not heard of God's law and other stories about His leadership for people like Abraham, Isaac, and Jacob. But she knew Yahweh's power and saving mercy toward His people in bringing them out of slavery. Through the message that she heard, she received saving faith. How do we know she had saving faith? We don't have to guess. We read in Hebrews 11:31: *"By faith Rahab the prostitute did not perish with those who were disobedient, because she had given a friendly welcome to the spies."* She's in the "Faith Hall of Fame" of Hebrews 11.

How did Rahab demonstrate her faith—her trust in God? First, she put her life on the line. What would have happened to her and her family if someone had discovered her giving support to the Hebrews? They would undoubtedly have tortured her and her family and then executed them. Rahab risked everything! And, in risking everything, she found Yahweh completely trustworthy. Second, Rahab repudiated her own past and her own people. When the Jews attacked, the slaughter would be complete—no mercy would be given. Her trust was transferred from the impregnable fortress and its people—created things—to the One who created the universe and everything in it.

Finally, we know that Rahab's faith was real because Rahab became identified with God's people. Her citizenship changed. Rahab, the Amorite prostitute, became a Jew, even a spiritual Jew, and not just a nominal Jew. She was accepted as a full-fledged member of the community. Then, of all things, she married Salmon, a prince of Judah! In Numbers 7:11-12 we read: *"And the LORD said to Moses, 'They shall offer their offerings, one chief each day, for the dedication of the altar.' He who offered his offering the first day was Nahshon the son of Amminadab, of the tribe of Judah."* Nahshon was the father of Salmon, the future husband of Rahab the former prostitute. Salmon, through his wife Rahab, was the father of Boaz, who was the father of Jesse, who was David the king's father. Another King would one day come from David's line—even Jesus the Christ.

Are we willing to die for the Gospel? For Christ? More importantly, will we live for Him? Are we willing to give up our old citizenship as members of the kingdom of darkness and join with our brothers and sisters in the Kingdom of light—His Church? That is what faith in Christ does. It moves us to action. It moves us to take risks for Him. No example of a living faith is more powerful than that of the prostitute Rahab, who gave up everything to trust wholly in

Yahweh and was placed in the lineage of Jesus. And the list of those who trusted wholeheartedly in the Creator God goes on and on.

Daniel and His Friends in Babylon

If one biblical character stands out for his complete and wholehearted trust in the true God, it must be Daniel. Imagine being carried off by an invading army and taken far from your home, place of worship, friends, and the way of life you've known ever since you were born. The invading hordes have destroyed the culture in which you have been living all your life. You have been swept away through no fault of your own. You would be devastated! It's an unimaginable disruption of all that is sacred and good about life. No longer would you be able to worship in the place that you hold dear. No longer would you be free to choose your own direction in life. You were now a slave with all freedoms lost.

Many of those who move to a foreign country today experience "culture shock." It's exciting to visit a new country for a short time, but as the days and weeks go by, many foreign settlers begin to feel lost and without a center or ground. It's sort of an emotional weightlessness. The old ways they have known for years suddenly are greatly missed. They may become depressed, even physically ill. But at least these cross-cultural businesspeople or missionaries have *chosen* to move. Not so with Daniel and those who were carried off as slaves into Babylon, not knowing what was in store for them in the future, not knowing if they would ever return to their homes, not knowing whether or not they would be executed. They had no freedom to do as they chose, but only what they were commanded to do by others.

Daniel was an exceptional man, both intellectually and spiritually. When commanded to eat only the king's food and drink his wine, Daniel displayed great tact and humility. He asked that a test be conducted. In Daniel 1:11-15 we read:

> "Then Daniel said to the steward whom the chief of the eunuchs had assigned over Daniel, Hananiah, Mishael, and Azariah, "Test your servants for ten days; let us be given vegetables to eat and water to drink. Then let our appearance and the appearance of the youths who eat the king's food be observed by you, and deal with your servants according to what you see." So he listened to them in this matter, and tested them for ten days. At the end of ten days it was

seen that they were better in appearance and fatter in flesh than all the youths who ate the king's food."

The guard, of course, was taking a big chance by agreeing to do what Daniel suggested. He could have been punished severely by his superiors. (We're told in the text that Yahweh was instrumental in his consent.) Nevertheless, we see that Daniel refused to accept the culture of Babylon. He followed Yahweh completely. He wasn't feeling sorry for himself or intimidated by his circumstances. Not at all! He had settled the matter entirely. No matter what the cost, he and his three friends—Shadrach, Meshach, and Abednego—would trust in the LORD with all their heart.

After three years of training, Daniel and the others entered the king's service. The first thing we see in Daniel chapter 2 is that King Nebuchadnezzar had a dream so vivid and disturbing that he couldn't sleep. So he called all his wise men—his magicians, enchanters, sorcerers and astrologers. They were to come and not only interpret the dream, but first to describe the dream itself! After failing to get his own "wise men" to tell him his dream, Nebuchadnezzar decides to put to death all the magicians, enchanters, sorcerers and astrologers in the kingdom. That includes Daniel and his friends. It's an unthinkable situation. The king has demanded what is impossible for a human being to perform.

When Daniel hears of the king's terrible plan, he goes immediately to his three friends. What do they do? They seek Yahweh in prayer. They know that He is the only One who can answer the king's command. In response to their faithful prayers, the LORD gives them the dream and its interpretation. Daniel then offers up to God this song of praise:

> *"Blessed be the name of God forever and ever,*
> *to whom belong wisdom and might.*
> *He changes times and seasons;*
> *he removes kings and sets up kings;*
> *he gives wisdom to the wise*
> *and knowledge to those who have understanding;*
> *he reveals deep and hidden things;*
> *he knows what is in the darkness,*
> *and the light dwells with him.*

To you, O God of my fathers,
I give thanks and praise,
for you have given me wisdom and might,
and have now made known to me what we asked of you,
for you have made known to us the king's matter"
(Daniel 2:19-23).

We won't dissect every little part of Daniel's song of praise and thanksgiving, but I commend it to you for your memorization for times of trouble and even despair, or when you are tempted to trust in things other than the living God. Notice first that *"wisdom and power"* are God's alone. It is Yahweh who controls the future, setting up kings, and then deposing them at His sovereign will (see Daniel 2:20-21 for instance). If God has that kind of power—and He does—will not our heavenly Father God help us in our time of trouble? It may not be the answer we expect or ask for, but it will always, always, always be according to his wisdom and loving-kindness. As David said in our beloved Psalms 23:4: *"Even though I walk through the valley of the shadow of death, I will fear no evil, for you are with me; your rod and your staff, they comfort me."* Or as Job said in Job 13:15: *"Though he slay me, I will hope in him…"*

Notice that God knows the secrets of the darkened, sinful hearts of all men and women. He sees into the darkness of sinful minds. He is *"the light"* of John 1:2-5: *"[Christ] was in the beginning with God. All things were made through him, and without him was not any thing made that was made. In him was life, and the life was the light of men. The light shines in the darkness, and the darkness has not overcome it."* For the Christian, God's omniscience—His ability to know and record even the deepest secrets of the hearts of men and women—is a wonderful certainty. But for the unbeliever, this truth reveals a God who is more like a heavenly peeping Tom. They hate the very idea of an omniscient God! But we are comforted, knowing that our gracious heavenly Father knows our needs even before they arise in us (Matthew 6:8).

You know the rest of the story. Daniel tells the king precisely what his dream was and gives him the interpretation from the LORD. The Babylonian government gives Daniel, like Joseph before him, a high position in the government. His three friends also receive high honors. Nebuchadnezzar, while falling at Daniel's feet following the LORD's revelation, nevertheless continues in his megalomania. He orders that a giant golden statue of himself be set up, and orders that everyone who doesn't fall down and worship it be thrown into a blazing furnace. Daniel's friends refuse to do so. Appearing before the king, they say, *"If this be so, our God whom we serve is able to deliver us from the burning fiery furnace, and he will deliver us out of your hand, O king. But if not, be it known to you, O king, that we will not serve your gods or worship the golden image that you have set up"* (Daniel 3:17-18). The soldiers then cast them into the furnace, which is so hot that the men who cast them in are themselves incinerated.

But Shadrach, Meshach and Abednego survive. Looking into the furnace from a distance, Nebuchadnezzar says, *"But I see four men unbound, walking in the midst of the fire, and they are not hurt; and the appearance of the fourth is like a son of the gods"* (Daniel 3:25). Who was that fourth man? I believe it was the pre-incarnate Christ—the Angel of the LORD. The three had trusted God even in the midst of their ordeal, and exited unscathed. But even if they were to have been executed, their trust in God remained firm.

Another king, Darius the Mede, would soon replace Nebuchadnezzar and his successor, Belshazzar. Meanwhile, Daniel continued to attract the wrath of the king's courtiers. At their request, the king published an edict *"...whoever makes petition to any god or man for thirty days, except to you, O king, shall be cast into the den of lions"* (Daniel 6:7). Daniel refused to worship some false god and continued to pray to the LORD three times a day. He was thrown into the den of hungry lions. But God shut the lions' mouths and Daniel survived. Soldiers then threw his betrayers to the huge cats which easily chewed them to pieces.

Daniel and his three friends trusted in the LORD with all their hearts, even in the midst of life and death situations, and leaned not on their own understanding of their difficult circumstances. We must understand that God may not save us physically from a fiery death or from the mouths of lions. Many today are being martyred for their faith in Christ. But we need not fear because our God is trustworthy even in death. What other god can claim the same? What other god would come to earth as a man and save his people from eternal death? None. Only Jesus.

More Old and New Testament Saints

In the Old Testament we read of faithful and courageous women like Deborah, Ruth, Naomi, Hannah, and Esther, and God-trusting men like Moses, Joshua, David, Elijah, Elisha, Isaiah, Jeremiah, and Nehemiah. In the New Testament we read of Mary, Elizabeth, Martha, her sister Mary, Mary Magdalene, and many more. Fellows like the eleven disciples, (the twelve minus Judas), then Paul, Barnabas and Timothy gave up everything to follow Christ. Men and women throughout the Bible lived on the edge, courting death and difficulty at every turn—taking huge risks to follow Jesus.

What can we say about them? Did their lives count for something? Absolutely. Without their steadfastness in the face of peril, ours would be a bankrupt faith today. Christianity is an historical faith, the truth of which is borne out over the years by those who have gone before us.

These saints lived for Jesus, but along with that, these men and women of faith lived for us! We are the beneficiaries of their lives. Like them, will my life and your life benefit those who will follow in our footsteps? Or will we shirk our commitment to be faithful to the One who is constantly and consistently faithful to us? One of my favorite verses is in that wonderful "Faith Hall of Fame"—Hebrews 11. In verses 24 through 27 we read:

> "By faith Moses, when he was grown up, refused to be called the son of Pharaoh's daughter, choosing rather to be mistreated with the people of God than to enjoy the fleeting pleasures of sin. He considered the reproach of Christ greater wealth than the treasures of Egypt, for he was looking to the reward. By faith he left Egypt, not being afraid of the anger of the king, for he endured as seeing him who is invisible."

True faith—saving faith—is to disregard mistreatment and disgrace and the things of this world for that which can never fail nor lapse—the eternal promises of an almighty and gracious God.

Trusting the Lord for Our Day-to-Day Needs

We've looked at men and women of faith and their solid trust in God in real life and death situations. But what about our mundane day-to-day lives? Can we trust the Lord to lead and guide us every moment of every day? Many of us, while spending Sunday morning worshiping and praising the one true God, then revert to what may be called "functional atheism." We forget about the God who claims to love us and look out for our well-being. I'm one of those people, as I struggle to recognize the LORD's sovereignty in my daily life. Let me tell you of one such struggle.

Stop Light Theology

Stop lights are not my friends. Well, I like stoplights when they're green, but I hate them when they turn red and I am actually forced to stop. Why? Because I have my agenda planned out for the day and I am frustrated when something changes it. In other words, deep down, I want my own way and I am frustrated when something happens to collide with my agenda. This frustration manifests itself in many ways, but one of those ways was in the simple, yet formerly frustrating, red light. I was a functional "Stop Light Atheist." Even though trusting God for my needs, I was functioning as if He didn't exist. But that's not true of me any more since I discovered "Stop Light Theology."

As I thought about red lights and my frustration that they require my obedience, I began to think about God's sovereignty. I began to wonder if God had planned for me to stop. Did He actually orchestrate my arriving at the stoplight just as it turned red? If He's absolutely sovereign over His creation, then the answer has to be "yes." If God's providence—His sovereign foresight and will to govern His creation—are true as the Bible says they are, the answer *had* to be "yes." Remember these verses from Galatians 4:4-5? *"But when the fullness of time had come, God sent forth his Son, born of woman, born under the law, to redeem those who were under the law, so that we might receive adoption as sons."* What does Paul mean, *"when the fullness of time had come?"* He means that Jesus was born into this world at the precise instant and in the exact place set by God the Father before the world began and as predicted precisely by the prophets, such as Isaiah and others. God's timing and knowledge is perfect. (More of God's attributes in chapter 3).

Joseph's Testimony of God's Sovereignty

We've already spoken of this man, Joseph. He is truly one of the great characters in redemptive history. And, as surely as he is a great patriarch of the Church, Joseph can also teach us a thing or two about "Stop Light Theology." <u>You remember that Joseph was sold into slavery in Egypt by his half-brothers</u>. He faced persecution and incarceration, yet was lifted up by Pharaoh to the second in command in the country. Later, as his felonious brothers trembled before his great authority, we read these words in Genesis 50:18-20:

> "His brothers also came and fell down before him and said, 'Behold, we are your servants.' But Joseph said to them, 'Do not fear, for am I in the place of God? As for you, you meant evil against me, but **God meant it for good**, to bring it about that many people should be kept alive, as they are today.'"

We see a perfect example of heavenly fore-ordination in Joseph and his brothers. God used the brothers' sin to bring about good circumstances. Egypt and the house of Jacob were saved from the famine. In the same way, God orchestrated Jesus's life and ministry. The cross looked like a terrible travesty of justice (and it was) and a great tragedy, but it became the best and most significant event in world history! Am I making a leap to go from Jesus and Joseph to mere stop lights? I don't think so.

Isaiah's Testimony of God's Sovereignty

To understand what the prophet Isaiah said about God's control of our day-to-day needs, let's look at these verses in Isaiah 46:9-11:

> "I am God, and there is none like me, declaring the end from the beginning and from ancient times things not yet done, saying, 'My counsel shall stand, and I will accomplish all my purpose,' calling a bird of prey from the east, the man of my counsel from a far country. ***I have spoken, and I will bring it to pass; I have purposed, and I will do it.***"

What God is saying through Isaiah is simply, "I know the future because I ordain the future." The holy God cannot be the author of sin. Why? Because God cannot do anything that is not altogether righteous and just. Adam was created as a very good man (Genesis 1:31). But Adam was given free will that allowed him to choose both the evil and the good. He chose the former and plunged the world into the mess we see around us today. Nevertheless, God uses the sins of men and women to accomplish His good purposes. Think of how the sin of Joseph's brothers brought about a good purpose (Genesis 5:20). Think about how David's sin involving Bathsheba and Uriah the Hittite resulted in Psalm 51, one of our most revered Psalms. Can we understand how this works itself out in our day-to-day lives? It is very difficult, but like the Trinity, it is a truth that in many ways remains a mystery to us. We who are finite cannot fully comprehend the infinite. Then how can we be certain that it is true? Simply by faith. We know it is true simply by trusting God's Word that it is true. As the Apostle says in 2 Corinthians 5:7, *"For we live by faith, not by sight."*

Since I've discovered this truth, my "red lights" have become an occasion for thanksgiving. Perhaps God has saved me from an accident down the road. Perhaps they are there to test me and help me to understand that He is in charge of even stoplights! Whatever the reason, I know that the red light is there for my benefit, and I can thank my heavenly Father for it. Whatever it is I can say as Paul does in 1 Thessalonians 5:16-18: *"Always be joyful. Continually be prayerful. In everything be thankful, because this is God's will in Christ Jesus for you."* Ask yourself, "How can anyone give thanks for wrongful circumstances in his or her life?" The answer has to be, "Because God has willed those circumstances to be so, and I know He loves me and has my best interests at heart." He is shaping me moment by moment into the likeness of His Son. That's His purpose, (Romans 8:29), and it has become my purpose too.

We'll deal more with this subject of God's absolute sovereignty in Chapter 3, where we'll investigate further the God who rules in sovereign majesty. Just suffice it to say here that our God is a gracious and loving heavenly Father. He's a Father like no other. He only brings good gifts, and He's the only real "promise keeper." God can keep His promises to us because He controls all events. He's absolutely sovereign. Otherwise, we would never be certain that even difficult times are in His hands. Yes, we can trust our loving heavenly Father as Job did in Job 13:15: *"Though [God] slay me, I will hope in him..."* And remember Paul's amazing and comforting words in Romans 8:28: *"And we know that for those who love God all things work together for good, for those who are called according to his purpose."* Therefore, we can trust Him fully for every daily need, even the little things like red lights!

Trusting God's Word ... My Bible

How can we know that God exists? Paul says in Romans 1:20: *"For his invisible attributes, namely, his eternal power and divine nature, have been clearly perceived, ever since the creation of the world, in the things that have been made. So they are without excuse."* One way we can know God exists is because we can see His handiwork in creation. But how can we know what He is like, what His plans are for the world, what His plans are for me? Only the Scriptures—God's holy Word—can answer these questions. Trusting God means trusting God's Word. Ours is the God who speaks, and He speaks to us through His eternal, inerrant, all-sufficient Word.

We live in an age of skepticism and of irrationality, even among many who call themselves "Christians." Remember when Jesus was on trial before Pontius Pilate? We read these words in John 18:36-38:

> *"Jesus answered, 'My kingdom is not of this world. If my kingdom were of this world, my servants would have been fighting, that I might not be delivered over to the Jews. But my kingdom is not from the world.' Then Pilate said to him, 'So you are a king?' Jesus answered, 'You say that I am a king. For this purpose I was born and for this purpose I have come into the world—to bear witness to the truth. Everyone who is of the truth listens to my voice.' Pilate said to him, 'What is truth?'"*

In much the same way, people today are likely to parrot Pilate and scornfully ask, "What is truth?" As we said earlier, the Enlightenment age of philosophers Immanuel Kant and David Hume was one of budding materialism. Their philosophy brought in a way of thinking that excluded the supernatural. Today, we face another, quite opposite philosophy, that of existentialism and even nihilism. These are philosophies of subjectivism. For the existentialist or nihilist so-called "truth" relies upon an individual's own viewpoint. In other words, the focus in the latter half of the 20th century changed from the rational to the irrational. Our culture has moved from materialism, which called for absolutes of what could be observed through the five senses, to the age of no absolutes, where any so-called transcendent, objective "truth" is called into question.

Have you ever heard someone say, "Well, that may be true for you, but it's not true for me"? Truth has become relative to one's own worldview. Even in Christendom many are saying about the Bible, "Well, I know that's what the Bible apparently says, but it only becomes truth for me as I understand it." In other words, individuals have become the final arbiters of what is and isn't true. The Bible has become for many not the receptacle and revelation of ultimate truth, but merely a carrier of "truths" to be individually selected. It's up to each person, then, to find out what is or isn't true for him or her. This subjective irrationality has infiltrated the Church to a major degree and is devastating to trusting God. We'll speak more of this in Chapter 2.

Here's the problem. While perhaps believing that Jesus Christ actually came in the flesh and is fully God and fully man, many deny His statement to Pontius Pilate that we've quoted above, as well as other biblical truths, such as His statement in John 14:6, *"I am the way and the truth and the life."* In fact, in the NIV translation, Jesus uses the term "the truth" ninety times, such as in *"I tell you the truth."* Now, if Jesus is truly God and He believes that truth exists apart from human understanding and observation, how can we not believe that He states the truth and nothing but the truth? Jesus said in His great high priestly prayer of John 17:17: *"Sanctify them in the truth; your word is truth."* And again in John 10:35 Jesus says, *"...the Scripture cannot be broken..."* If we worship Christ as God, how can we not believe what He tells us in His Word? To say otherwise is simply unbelief!

The point of all this is that we ***can*** believe Jesus. He does speak the truth! Biblical Christianity has always believed the Bible to be inerrant in its original languages. Notice where attacks against God's Word focus in today's post–modern, irrational age—in the book of Genesis. The theory of evolution has become for the majority a "fact" that has been supposedly "proven" by scientific inquiry. But if a person of moderate intelligence thinks about evolution for one or two minutes, he will see that it is totally irrational. First, you have to completely discard the very basic scientific truth of causation. Every effect has to have a cause. But atheistic evolution denies causation saying that so-called "chance" is the cause of all that exists. But "chance" is merely the odds of something happening, like a flipped coin turning up heads fifty-percent of the time. Chance has no power to create anything. The likelihood of complex improvements in life forms "by accident" is so low it is laughable. It's like the proverbial explosion in a print factory that produced "Gone With the Wind."

Another basic question is about origins. "Why is there something rather than nothing?" The most basic truth is stated in Latin, "*Ex nihilo nihil fit*"—"out of nothing nothing comes." The universe did not create itself. For something to create itself, it would have to exist before it existed, which is impossible! Unbelievers willfully forget that the reason—the only reason—something exists today is that something or someone has the power of existence within itself, or Himself. That someone is Jesus Christ! He has existed from all eternity and all life has come from Him. Notice what Jesus says in John 5:26: *"For as the Father has life in himself, so he has granted the Son also to have life in himself."* This is what Jesus means when He says in John 14:6, *"I am the life..."*

I believe that the creation vs. evolution debate is an historical argument and not a scientific one. I want to trust someone who was there as an eyewitness. According to the Scriptures, there is Someone who was there. John 1:1-3 says, *"In the beginning was the Word, and the Word was with God, and the Word was God. He was in the beginning with God. All things were made through him, and without him was not any thing made that was made."* John, speaking under the auspices of the Holy Spirit, goes on to say in 1:14, *"And the Word became flesh and dwelt among us, and we have seen his glory, glory as of the only Son from the Father, full of grace and truth."* The pre-incarnate Christ was there, and we can believe Him, because He *is* the truth.

Though this book isn't meant to provide evidence for the Christian faith, there are many others that do so in such a way that we can be confident that God's Word is completely reliable. Such confidence is crucial, since unless we understand and agree that the Bible is a book of ultimate truth, we will never be able to trust in the One who, by His Spirit, caused it to come into existence through the pens of his appointed men over thousands of years, yet without error or contradiction. If we can't trust God's Word, we'll never trust God and the many promises that He makes to us. The Bible is God's Word and He wouldn't lie to us. God doesn't lie. God can't do anything that is counter to His altogether righteous character. His promises are true and He has the power and the sovereign will to bring them to pass. Knowing that our heavenly Father made promises to us through His Word, and that He keeps His promises, is crucial to His command that we, His people, *"Trust in the LORD with all your heart..."*

God's Promises Seem Too Good To Be True

I stated earlier that Proverbs 3:5&6 were my favorite verses in Scripture. Now I have to say that that's not entirely true. For me, it's a toss-up between those verses and Genesis 15:17: *"When the sun had gone down and it was dark, behold, a smoking fire pot and a flaming torch passed between these pieces."* I guess you might say that Genesis 15:17 is the reason that Proverbs 3:5&6 are my favorite verses in the Bible. I'm certain by this time you are totally confused! "Beasley, have you lost your happy mind?" No, I haven't. Let me explain.

Genesis 15 is one of the greatest chapters in the Bible. It is where the Gospel of salvation by grace alone through faith alone is first made known. In Genesis 15:6, we have this amazing statement: *"And he believed the LORD, and [God] counted it to him as righteousness."* Abram trusted Yahweh's promises to him and Yahweh imputed or reckoned Abram as righteous on the basis of his faith alone. Abram's righteous standing before God wasn't based on his own good works or anything that he did. It was all based on what Yahweh was willing to do for Abram! It is sometimes called the Abrahamic covenant, God's promise that was never abrogated or replaced by God's covenant through Moses where the Law was later introduced. It is still in effect today, even though it has been enhanced and clarified through the New Covenant instituted through Jesus Christ's shed blood.

But Abram's faith wasn't complete, or wholehearted. He needed reassurance that God's promises were absolutely trustworthy. So Abram asked God for more proof. A reasonable thing to do, wasn't it? He says of the promised land in Genesis 15:8, *"O Lord GOD, how am I to know that I shall possess it?"* So God told

Abram to gather up some animals and birds. Abram cut up the animals according to Yahweh's orders, and placed the pieces and the dead birds opposite one another so that a path was formed down the middle. Immediately, Abram fell into a deep sleep. Then, *"When the sun had gone down and it was dark, behold, a smoking fire pot and a flaming torch passed between these pieces."* What in the world is happening?

In the ancient near east, when a king or other large landholder wanted to ensure that his vassals or subjects were loyal to him, he would order them to make such an arrangement of dead animals and birds. Then, he would require his subjects to walk through the pieces. In doing so, they were saying, in effect, "If we do not carry out all our promises to you, to provide you with food and to help you in battle, you may do to us what we have done to these animals and birds." In other words, the vassals and subjects took an oath unto death!

But what about this smoking fire-pot and burning torch? They are what is called a "theophany," a visible manifestation of the invisible God. You will recall that when Yahweh brought the Hebrews out of slavery in Egypt, He led them in a pillar of fire and a pillar of cloud. As Nehemiah recalls in Nehemiah 9:12, *"By a pillar of cloud you led them in the day, and by a pillar of fire in the night to light for them the way in which they should go."* So this *"...smoking fire-pot [and] blazing torch..."* are physical manifestations—theophanies—of Yahweh, the pre-incarnate Christ. The pre-incarnate Christ is found throughout the Old Testament Scriptures. Many times He appears as *"the Angel of the LORD"* as in Genesis 16:7-11, where He speaks to Sarah's servant Hagar. Over all, the phrase, *"The Angel of the LORD"* appears 60 times in the Hebrew Scriptures.

What has happened is that while Abram is sound asleep, the LORD Himself has passed through the pieces and sworn an oath unto death. In doing this God said, in effect, "If I do not fulfill my promises to you, and even if you don't fulfill your promises to me, you may do to me what you have done to these animals and birds." God Himself took the oath unto death! Many years later, *"...when the fullness of time had come, God sent forth his Son, born of woman, born under the law, to redeem those who were under the law, so that we might receive adoption as sons."* (Galatians 4:4-5). Yahweh's oath looked ahead to the day when He would stand upon the earth and die to take away the sins of His people in His death on the cross. Jesus Christ confirmed and perfected the covenant with Abraham that God had unilaterally made thousands of years before, when *"a smoking fire pot and a flaming torch passed between these pieces."*

The writer to the Hebrews says it like this:

> *"For people swear by something greater than themselves, and in all their disputes an oath is final for confirmation. So when God desired to show more convincingly to the heirs of the promise the unchangeable character of his purpose, he guaranteed it with an oath, so that by* **two unchangeable things***, in which it is impossible for God to lie, we who have fled for refuge might have strong encouragement to hold fast to the hope set before us. We have this as a sure and steadfast anchor of the soul, a hope that enters into the inner place behind the curtain, where Jesus has gone as a forerunner on our behalf..."* (Hebrews 6:16-20a).

The *"two unchangeable things"* are God's promise and His subsequent oath to Abraham. The patriarch's doubt produced for his spiritual offspring an absolutely certain hope, that salvation rests not upon our promises to God, but upon His promises to us. Our salvation as Abraham's spiritual descendants rests completely upon God and not upon us. What could be greater than such a certain rescue? That's the Gospel in a nutshell.

So, what does God promise to those who trust Him? We know of course that first and foremost, God promises eternal life for all who trust in Him. Recall these familiar words from John 3:16-18:

> *"For God so loved the world that he gave his one and only Son, that whoever believes in him shall not perish but have eternal life. For God did not send his Son into the world to condemn the world, but to save the world through him. Whoever believes in him is not condemned, but whoever does not believe stands condemned already because they have not believed in the name of God's one and only Son."*

Just as Abraham was saved through faith, we, too, are eternally saved through simple, child-like faith—trust—in what the person and work of Jesus has done for us. At the same time, as God through His Spirit exchanges our old stony heart for one of flesh (Ezekiel 11:19), convicts us of sin, and we repent before Him, our new lives in Christ begin. We have eternal benefits right away! Ours is not a "pie-in-the-sky" faith. Believers have eternal life ***now***! We have the great promises of God, **now**! "OK," someone asks, "What are the promises?" They are so many and so far-reaching that many books have been written on them. That said, here are but a few of God's promises to those who put their trust in Him. They all have some overlap, and I have listed them in no particular order:

A Certain Hope for the Future

Hebrews chapter 11 begins with this definition of faith: *"Now faith is confidence in what we hope for and assurance about what we do not see."* In other words, faith in Christ brings a guaranteed hope of eternal life with God, a hope that is currently in the future and invisible. Some churches would deny that a Christian can have absolute assurance of salvation, arguing that assurance of salvation only leads to an overconfidence in one's abilities to persevere.

But both the Old and New Testaments argue solidly against this teaching. We **can** have a certain hope. It is even incumbent on us to have absolute assurance of our salvation! If we don't, then we are trusting in our own "good works" to save us. If we rest in our works, we will either become disillusioned if we fail or self-righteous if we think we're good enough. Instead, it is Christ who provides full salvation and hangs on to His loved ones through all of life.

Just think of Psalms 23:6: *"Surely your goodness and love will follow me all the days of my life, and I will dwell in the house of the LORD forever."* Or Paul, who liked to shout the doctrine from the rooftops, said in Romans 8:38-39: *"For I am sure that neither death nor life, nor angels nor rulers, nor things present nor things to come, nor powers, nor height nor depth, nor anything else in all creation, will be able to separate us from the love of God in Christ Jesus our Lord."* If the Apostle Paul is sure, then we can be too. One of the great benefits of serving God in this life is the perfect assurance that we will be with Him for eternity.

A Life of Eternal Purpose

I'm approaching the day when I will leave this phase of my eternal life. Many folks my age are depressed because they feel worthless—without a central purpose in life. They may have retired from a career or from raising a family, endeavors that gave them a real sense of purpose. Now all that is behind them, leaving them without goals or aspirations. But for the elderly Christian man or woman, indeed for Christians of all ages, God has given us a real sense of purpose in life that never fades. Our purpose is to glorify God by enjoying Him and allowing Him to change us into the likeness of His Son—our Lord Jesus. We are given the incredibly important job of continuing in Christ's work of calling out a people of His own and instructing them in righteousness. After his wonderful statement in Ephesians 2:8-9 that we are saved by grace alone through faith alone, the Apostle Paul goes on to say in verse 10: *"For we are his workmanship, created in Christ Jesus for good works, which God prepared beforehand, that we should walk in them."*

I recall the old joke that "Some people are born just to serve as bad examples for the rest of us." Not so for the Christian. We are given work to do that will have eternal consequences. We belong to an organization—Christ's Church—that is the only organization with a future! I may die someday soon, but my life isn't over—it's actually just beginning. Death for the Christian is merely the passageway into real life. The only thing we lose is the ability to sin. Therefore, I know that everything I do for Christ, every day I wake up to serve Him, has eternal purpose. It counts forever. My purpose is to glorify God by living for Him.

Think about it. Jesus said in Mark 9:41: *"For truly, I say to you, whoever gives you a cup of water to drink because you belong to Christ will by no means lose his reward."* Even a cup of cold water given in Christ's name has eternal consequences. Though these good works aren't earning our salvation, they are the evidence of saving faith and they will be rewarded. God will reward His sheep bountifully even though we don't deserve any reward. God crowns His own works through us with eternal glory for His children. Absolutely no other endeavor in life can promise such purpose and eternal benefits.

A Life of Rest and Contentment

One of God's most precious gifts to His children is that of rest and contentment. In fact, it's what the phrase *"Trust in the LORD with all your heart"* is all about. As we'll see in Chapter 2, to trust in any other thing than the true and living God and His gospel of grace, is to promote unrest and discontent. Only the true God can bring us rest and full contentment. Jesus calls us to rest in Him in Matthew

11:28-30: *"Come to me, all who labor and are heavy laden, and I will give you rest. Take my yoke upon you, and learn from me, for I am gentle and lowly in heart, and you will find rest for your souls. For my yoke is easy, and my burden is light."* Jesus isn't talking about His flock just kicking back in our easy chairs and not rolling up our sleeves and working. Neither is He saying that we should just accept the *status quo* in our family, church, neighborhood, or community.

What He's talking about is that if we trust in Him alone for our everyday needs and eternal security, we can cease to worry and fret over the future. Jesus is in full command of every eventuality, and His way is the best way.

Some Christians believe that God is fully capable of saving them, and are assured that He saves by His grace alone through faith in Christ. But they wonder, "If I'm saved, why do I keep on thinking evil thoughts and even doing some unrighteous deeds?" I have a student-friend in Ukraine who struggles with this. When counseling him, I always go through the objective reality of his salvation. He completely believes that Christ came in human flesh and that He suffered, died, and rose again. He believes God's promises in the Bible are all true. Then I go through some subjective proofs and he agrees. He loves to worship God, to study God's Word, and to have fellowship with God's people. "But" he always says, "I'm such a sinner!" I laugh and assure him that being a sinner is the only qualification for God's kingdom. Jesus came to call sinners, not the righteous, to repentance (Luke 5:31). When we mourn over our continuing sinfulness and strive to confess our sin, repent and be changed, it is strong evidence of our salvation.

St. Augustine rightly said that all Christians are both saved and sinners—both justified and yet retaining the sin nature. The apostle John says in 1 John 1:8, *"If we say we have no sin, we deceive ourselves, and the truth is not in us."* But John goes on to say in verse 9, *"If we confess our sins, he is faithful and just to forgive us our sins and to cleanse us from all unrighteousness."* Even in the midst of our sin and failure, Jesus stands ready to forgive and cleanse His children. We can and do have full assurance that Jesus will neither leave us nor forsake us (Hebrews 13:5b).

A Life of Present Security

When Moses reached 120 years of age and the people of God were about to enter the Promised Land, we read this of his actions in Deuteronomy 31:7-8:

> *"Then Moses summoned Joshua and said to him in the sight of all Israel, "Be strong and courageous, for you shall go with this people into the land that the LORD has sworn to their fathers to give them, and you shall put them in possession of it. It is the LORD who goes before you. He will be with you; he will not leave you or forsake you. Do not fear or be dismayed."*

We should never take our eyes off of the fact that "*the LORD*" here is none other than the Lord Jesus Christ before He came to this earth in human flesh and blood. He is Yahweh, the great "I AM WHO I AM" of the burning bush of Exodus 3:14. And, as the writer to the Hebrews says in 13:8, *"Jesus Christ is the same yesterday and today and forever."* Jesus Himself tells us in John 14:1-3: *"Let not your hearts be troubled. Believe in God; believe also in me. In my Father's house are many rooms. If it were not so, would I have told you that I go to prepare a place for you? And if I go and prepare a place for you, I will come again and will take you to myself, that where I am you may be also."* Does Jesus mean that we'll never have trials and trouble in this world? Not at all. He is saying that you have eternal security and can experience true rest and contentment now in the midst of the evil and tribulation of the world. Nothing can happen to us that our gracious and all–merciful God has not ordained.

I have encountered lots of trouble in my life, as I'm certain you have also.(Or if you haven't yet, you will!) One consequence of the troubles I've faced has been difficulty sleeping. In those times I remember what Jesus said in the Great Commission of Matthew 28:18, *"All authority in heaven and on earth has been given to me."* The Greek word used for "authority" here is *exousian*, which means "power." **All** authority and power is given to the God-man who loves us and gave His life to save us. Jesus ends the Great Commission with the words, *"And behold, I am with you always, to the end of the age."* Worry, unrest, false guilt, and discontent go out the window when we rest completely in Him. In fact, I've counted the command not to be anxious or afraid or worried 19 times in the New Testament, most by the Lord Himself.

One of the best things about growing older is that we can look back and see the many times that the Lord has acted on our behalf in times of trouble. What joy in knowing that even in times of stress, frustration, sadness, and great difficulty, God has our back.

A Life of Fulfilled Needs

Paul gives us this promise in Philippians 4:19: *"And my God will supply every need of yours according to his riches in glory in Christ Jesus."* And remember Jesus speaks to God's provision in the Sermon on the Mount where He says:

> *"Therefore do not be anxious, saying, 'What shall we eat?' or 'What shall we drink?' or 'What shall we wear?' For the Gentiles seek after all these things, and your heavenly Father knows that you need them all. But seek first the kingdom of God and his righteousness, and all these things will be added to you. "Therefore do not be anxious about tomorrow, for tomorrow will be anxious for itself. Sufficient for the day is its own trouble"* (Matthew 6:31-34).

In fact, as I mentioned above, the most oft repeated command of Jesus is "don't worry." In His wonderful miracles of the feeding of the 4,000 (Matthew 15), and the 5,000 (Mark 6), Jesus showed that He has the power to multiply provisions. From some fish and a few loaves, He fed the multitudes. I have witnessed such extraordinary providence in my own life. Perhaps you, too, have had an experience where God has worked in a mighty way to assist you. It is important to record those experiences and to remind ourselves of them in future times of need.

I lived most of my life in southern California, but in 1974 my real estate development business took me and my family to live in Florida for a few years. I had gotten into financial difficulty in 1973 when the market soured, and I intended to climb out of my situation by development opportunities in Florida. It was not to be. As a last attempt to have some success, I developed 12 single family lots on the first fairway of a golf course in 1979. But without warning, the real estate market took another turn for the worse. The bank was about to foreclose on the development loan I had acquired from them. My family had returned to California and I was all alone in our home which I couldn't sell. My back was to the wall. I had nowhere to turn but to God. Sitting all alone in an empty house, I prayed.

As I was praying, the telephone rang. It was an acquaintance from Los Angeles whom I had met through a mutual friend. He knew that I was in the real estate business but knew nothing of my current situation. He said, "My aunt up in the San Fernando Valley has more money than sense. She called me this morning with a bee in her bonnet about buying some lots in South Florida. The only condition is that they have to be on a golf course." I immediately flew to Los Angeles and we closed the deal in two weeks, staving off foreclosure.

One of my close friends calls these times, "Holy Ghost Stories." He collects them. But someone asks, "What about Christians who have been murdered for their faith, or even starved to death?" Yes, there are times when God's providential care for His people seems to vanish. One needs only to remember Job's misery, how Satan took all he had, even his health. But for the great majority, God feeds us and clothes us, and gives us homes in which to live. We return thanks to Him for every provision in our lives (1 Corinthians 10:31).

We are children of Adam and live in a world that's cursed because of his sin and its devastating effects. We all suffer in many ways because of the noetic effects of sin. But even when it appears that God may have abandoned us, we know that it's not the end of the story. Like Job, the end result will be better than the beginning. Through it all, God is either strengthening us for future service, (see chapter 4), or calling us home to the joy of being with Him for eternity.

A Life of Peace—Shalom

According to *Strong's Concordance*, the Hebrew word *shalom* "means completeness, wholeness, health, peace, welfare, safety, soundness, tranquility, prosperity, perfectness, fullness, rest, harmony, the absence of agitation or discord. Shalom... means to be complete, perfect and full." This is *"the peace which surpasses all understanding"* (Philippians 4:7). *Shalom* is the word that Jesus uses when he says, *"Peace I leave with you; my peace I give to you. Not as the world gives do I give to you. Let not your hearts be troubled, neither let them be afraid."* (John 14:27). *Shalom* is the free gift of God. The people of the world long for such peace, such *shalom*. But to paraphrase a popular old country and western song, they are looking for *shalom* in all the wrong places.

Do we have peace—*shalom*—at all times? No, we still are sinners in a sinful world, and so we doubt God and suffer sleeplessness sometimes. Whenever I get to that point where the cares and concerns of this world are bearing heavily upon me, I remember Isaiah 61:3c: *"...and a garment of praise instead of a spirit of despair"* (NIV). I think of this verse and am driven to thanksgiving for all of God's mercy to me. My mind, focused on Him, then rests in His *shalom*.

A Life of Strength and Encouragement

The greatest gift that God gives His children for life in this present world is the gift of His Spirit who dwells within us. Before we came to know Christ savingly, we were without the ability to resist temptation. Oh, we might, by sheer power of our own wills, have a little strength. But God gives us all of His strength to stand firm against the world, the flesh, and the devil (Ephesians 6:13-14). Is there any greater strength than that which the LORD provides? As Isaiah summarizes it well:

> *"Have you not known? Have you not heard? The LORD is the everlasting God, the Creator of the ends of the earth. He does not faint or grow weary; his understanding is unsearchable. He gives power to the faint, and to him who has no might he increases strength. Even youths shall faint and be weary, and young men shall fall exhausted; but they who wait for the LORD shall renew their strength; they shall mount up with wings like eagles; they shall run and not be weary; they shall walk and not faint"* (Isaiah 40:28-31).

Paul adds to Isaiah, saying in 1 Corinthians 10:13: *"No temptation has overtaken you that is not common to man. God is faithful, and he will not let you be tempted beyond your ability, but with the temptation he will also provide the way of escape, that you may be able to endure it."* But Christ's strength also has positive application, and not just in keeping us from sin. God has given each of us work to do that he has appointed for us (Ephesians 2:10). And He will give us the strength to accomplish what He has ordained for us to do. He will also give us brothers and sisters who will stand with us in prayer and mutual support.

I often feel that I'm not capable or qualified to accomplish the tasks that I believe God has set before me. Do you ever feel the same way? We each need to remember when God asks us to do something, He also gives us the strength, capability, and encouragement to do it, if we trust Him to help. In the first part of the fifth century, the Bishop of Hippo in North Africa—the famous St. Augustine—prayed, "Oh God, grant what Thou commandest, and command what Thou dost desire..." In other words, "God, help me to do what you command, and command me to do anything you want." The prayer caused one of history's major conflicts in Christendom. A British monk named Pelagius believed that Christians were fully competent on their own and didn't need God's grace either for salvation or obedience. But Pelagius's views were condemned by the church and rightly so. We need the strength and courage that only God can provide for us, and He supplies those needs through the riches of His grace.

In 1 Corinthians 1:26-29, Paul speaks about who we are without God's strength:

> "For consider your calling, brothers: not many of you were wise according to worldly standards, not many were powerful, not many were of noble birth. But God chose what is foolish in the world to shame the wise; God chose what is weak in the world to shame the strong; God chose what is low and despised in the world, even things that are not, to bring to nothing things that are, so that no human being might boast in the presence of God."

Later on, Paul will say this about himself in 2 Corinthians 12:9-10:

> "But he said to me, "My grace is sufficient for you, for my power is made perfect in weakness." Therefore I will boast all the more gladly of my weaknesses, so that the power of Christ may rest upon me. For the sake of Christ, then, I am content with weaknesses, insults, hardships, persecutions, and calamities. For when I am weak, then I am strong."

For the Christian, weakness is strength. God works through weak people and He alone gives us the strength to do things we never thought we could do.

A Life of the Father's Discipline

I'm not a great fan of discipline. I would rather avoid it if I could. (Like red lights!) Although receiving Christ at an early age, I came to truly know Him somewhat later in life, and spent at least nineteen years under the Lord's discipling hand. It was not fun. I had all kinds of trouble—at home, in my business, and adjusting to His ways and allowing Him to get rid of my old ways. But as I look back on the experience, which mostly ended over 20 years ago, I wouldn't trade all the possessions in the world for it. God lovingly took me to the woodshed, as it were, gave me a much needed spanking, and changed me over those difficult years. Hebrews 12:7-8 tells us, *"It is for discipline that you have to endure. God is treating you as sons. For what son is there whom his father does not discipline? If you are left without discipline, in which all have participated, then you are illegitimate children and not sons."* I know beyond the shadow of a doubt that I am God's son, in part because of the discipline He took me through those many years ago. We need to remember that God doesn't punish His children, as we normally think of punishment. Discipline, as the writer to the Hebrews says, is all about His love for us—to equip us and to bring us joy. God's discipline brings us to a greater fellowship and trust in Him.

As a former elder in Christ's church, I, along with my fellow elders, was sometimes called upon to discipline a church member for some sin that has brought Christ's reputation into question. This is neither an easy nor a fun thing to do. But church discipline is one of the three marks of a true church along with preaching the Gospel and administration of the two Christ-given sacraments—Baptism and the Lord's Supper. When church discipline is administered it is not for revenge or to punish the offender. Discipline is always for the purpose of renewal and restoration to fellowship of those disciplined, and for God's honor and glory. As I look back on those years under the disciplining hand of my heavenly Father, I rejoice that He loved me enough to discipline me and set my feet on the right path.

The Spiritual and Intellectual Joy of God's Word

God has revealed Himself to mankind in two ways. The first, of which we've already spoken, is His creation. We call this God's "general revelation." This source of knowledge about God is common to all men everywhere. Paul speaks of it in Romans 1:18-20:

> *"For the wrath of God is revealed from heaven against all ungodliness and unrighteousness of men, who by their unrighteousness suppress the truth. For what can be known about God is plain to them, because God has shown it*

to them. For his invisible attributes, namely, his eternal power and divine nature, have been clearly perceived, ever since the creation of the world, in the things that have been made. So they are without excuse."

All men and women since creation have had this general revelation of God. But for God's people, there remains another "special revelation"—the Bible.

Paul gives us this truth about God's Word in 2 Timothy 3:16-17: *"All Scripture is breathed out by God and profitable for teaching, for reproof, for correction, and for training in righteousness, that the man of God may be complete, equipped for every good work."* The Bible is coming under increasing attack both from outside the church and within. Don't get sucked in to those who want to abuse it. Over thousands of years, God revealed Himself in an ever-expanding way as not only our Creator, but also as our Redeemer. From Genesis 1 through Revelation 22, the Bible has but one theme—the Lord Jesus Christ and His glorious promises to save His people from their sins. Not one word of the Scriptures is weightless. Every "jot and tittle" is given for our benefit and delight. As the psalmist says in Psalms 119:105, *"Your word is a lamp to my feet and a light to my path..."* We'll further discuss God's wonderful Word in Chapter 4.

God's written Word speaks of the history of what has gone before us and His plans for His creation's future. The Christian worldview—or framework through which we make sense of the world and the history of mankind—can be summed up in four words: Creation, Fall, Redemption, and Restoration. The world's history had a beginning and it will have an ending. History isn't circular as some eastern religions teach, it is linear and God's plan is to destroy this old earth and recreate it in righteousness (Isaiah 65:17a, Revelation 21:1). What intellectual joy there is in studying and knowing God's plan of redemption that has unfolded for over 6,000 years, and His purposes for our future with Him.

A Life of Freedom and Delight in Godly Wisdom

James 1:5 tells us, *"If any of you lacks wisdom, let him ask God, who gives generously to all without reproach, and it will be given him."* Godly wisdom is not like the wisdom of the world. In the world we're told to "Look out for Number 1!"—meaning ourselves. We're told by the world that wisdom consists of getting what we want out of life. But godly wisdom helps us to focus on God and others, walking according to God's will and way, and not our own. God's wisdom brings life and health and freedom from slavery to the world and its idolatrous ways. It's the only wisdom worth having, and God's Word is full of His wisdom for our help in this life.

The basis of Godly wisdom is God's law as abbreviated and focused in the Ten Commandments (Exodus 20:1-17, Deuteronomy 5:6-21). God saw how His people were suffering as slaves in Egypt and brought them out of slavery by His mighty hand. He then took them to Mt. Sinai and gave Moses these ten basic laws by which they were to live. God didn't take the Israelites out of slavery to enslave them again. Far from it! He brought them out and gave them His law that they might live free from the enslaving, sinful ways of the pagan tribes in the Promised Land. Left to ourselves, apart from the saving grace of our Lord, we want nothing to do with God's law. It's too restrictive! We want to be free to do our own thing—to live lives centered on self. But God created us to be like Himself and sent Jesus to restore us to His image. We're like the fish that sees the birds flying overhead and thinks to be truly free we need to fly. But God created fish to swim. A few minutes out of water, and fish die. To be truly free means to be what we were created to be—a people made in His image. God's law graciously shows us how.

The book of Proverbs is all about godly wisdom versus the wisdom of the world. It has been said to be "the Ten Commandments in shoe leather." I particularly love the first 9 chapters where a father seeks to convince his son that employing God's wisdom is the path to freedom from slavery to the world's ways. Study the book. Apply its wisdom to your life. It will put your feet on fruitful paths of righteousness for Christ's sake. In the final analysis, only two ways exist in life. The old radio preacher, Dr. J. Vernon McGee, used to say that life is like the Pasadena Freeway near his home. People are going two different ways: one to destruction and one to everlasting life. Trust that God alone provides the pathway on which to base our lives and be truly free (see chapter 4).

Freedom from the Fear of Death

We've already spoken about the Christian's freedom from fear earlier, but we need to address people's most all-consuming fear—the fear of death. Trust in Christ and His finished work on the cross should eliminate this fear completely. In Hebrews 2:14-15 we read:

> *"Since therefore the children share in flesh and blood, he himself likewise partook of the same things, that through death he might destroy the one who has the power of death, that is, the devil, and deliver all those who through fear of death were subject to lifelong slavery."*

In no uncertain terms, Christ's death and resurrection guarantee eternal life for all who trust Him. Our assurance of eternal life is not based on the amount or depth of our faith. It is the object of our faith—Jesus—who saves us. What joy that we Christians can face death with confidence, not fear.

My older brother, Bill, died recently. Like my own experience, Bill was baptized early in life, but it was twenty-five more years before God's Spirit opened his heart and he began to follow Christ. At that time, Bill was wandering aimlessly in life, his fear of death drowned out by his use of drugs and alcohol. Bill was a hedonist, always looking for the next fun-filled experience. But God grabbed hold of Bill and transformed him in an amazing way. He became a pastor and a missionary, extolling God's grace to anyone who would listen. His testimony to his old college friends just prior to his death was authentic and powerful. Bill faced a painful death with a big smile on his face, and with great anticipation of the eternal joy set before him. Bill trusted God's Word and joined with the Apostle Paul in saying, *"...thanks be to God, who gives us the victory through our Lord Jesus Christ!"* (1 Corinthians 15:57).

A Life of Freedom From Guilt and Shame

I've saved one of the best parts of being a Christian in the here-and-now until last. Saved by God's grace alone, we can feel relief that we are sinners. (A lesson my friend in Ukraine is finally learning!) We don't have to hide behind a "righteous" mask. I hate sin, and I want to strive more to be like Jesus, but I revel in Christ that even in the midst of my sin, my ungodliness, my rebellion, and enmity against Him, He uses even sin for my ultimate good. I know that as John says in 1 John 1:9: *"If we confess our sins, he is faithful and just to forgive us our sins and to cleanse us from all unrighteousness."*

When Satan tries to tell me that I'm guilty of some sin, even as far back as when I was not living for Christ, I just throw that verse back in his face. I go to sleep guilt free and awake guilt free. I have tried to live at peace with everyone, and have confessed my sin both to God and to other believers. I am free from guilt and shame. What a joyous benefit of God! If you struggle with guilt and shame because of your past or current sinful behavior or attitudes, memorize and always remember the wonderful declaration of Romans 8:1-2: *"There is therefore now no condemnation for those who are in Christ Jesus. For the law of the Spirit of life has set you free in Christ Jesus from the law of sin and death."* No condemnation now. No condemnation ever for those who are in Christ Jesus!

As I said, I hate the sin in my life. Because I recognize that I'm a sinner saved only by grace, I am actually looking forward to the day when I shall leave this old body and mind of sin—this sinful flesh—and be united with a new sinless body, with a new mind that thinks only high and righteous thoughts, and with a new tongue that says only good things. The gift of eternal life for this old sinner is a certain hope. So certain, in fact, that I've even written an epitaph for my grave stone.

> "Here lies a sinner man,
> selfish to the core.
> Gone to be with Jesus,
> gone to sin no more."

We've been speaking about God's wonderful gifts of purpose, hope, rest, fulfilled needs, freedom from our fears, and from guilt and shame. These gifts all culminate in the peace that passes all understanding—*shalom*. That peace comes only with the knowledge that one rests secure from the pounding and trauma of this old sinful world because of what Jesus Christ has done for us. Let's now move on to the second phrase of Proverbs 3:5—our own understanding—where we'll speak more about our old enemy—sin.

Questions for Reflection and Further Study

1. Read Psalm 64:10. What does the psalmist say is a principal result of trust in the

LORD? Does your Bible use another word for "trust" in there? What is it?

2. Read Proverbs 14:26. What does the phrase "fear of the LORD" mean to you? Of what benefits does the proverb speak? Just to the one who trusts, or others as well?

3. Read Isaiah 26:3. What does the prophet say is another benefit of trusting the LORD? Why would Isaiah come to that conclusion?

4. Read Jeremiah 17:7. Does this remind you of a Psalm of David? Which one? What benefits does Jeremiah give for the person who trusts in the LORD? Has the "heat" ever come into your life? What was it? How did the Lord work in that situation?

5. Read Nahum 1:7. How does Nahum express what God will do for those who put their trust in Him? What is a "stronghold" or "refuge?"

6. Read Mark 9:14-29. What promise does Jesus give to the father of the boy in verse 23? What do you think our Lord meant by "all things?" What request does the father make in verse 24? Is that a prayer you have ever uttered?

7. Read Romans 5:1. What benefits of trust in Christ does Paul mention here? What does he mean?

8. Read Galatians 3:1-14. Paul sets up two things that oppose one another. What are they? What have the Galatians been doing that Paul condemns? These opposing things have different origins or means in verse 3. What are they? Can you state the gospel clearly in your own words?

9. Read Hebrews 11:1. The ESV uses "assurance" and "conviction" to define faith. The King James uses "substance" and "evidence." What does your Bible say? What words do you think are most helpful? How would you define "faith" or "trust" in your own words?

10. Read 1 John 5:4. Who is it that has faith? What does this faith do according to John? What does this "victory" mean in your own life?

Chapter II
"And Do Not Lean On Your Own Understanding"

Throughout much of my life, I lived in San Diego, California. San Diego used to have a unique venue in Balboa Park where each summer outdoor musical comedies were performed. One of my favorite musicals that was produced from time-to time was *Annie Get Your Gun*. Annie Oakley sings a song in that musical that goes like this: "Folks are dumb where I come from, They ain't had any learning. Still they're happy as can be, Doin' what comes naturally." Now that may be a nice sentiment for Annie and unbelievers, but doing what comes naturally is, in truth, a curse.

Let's recall a conversation between our Lord and His disciples, particularly Simon Peter. Peter had just proclaimed Jesus to be *"...the Christ, the Son of the living God"* (Matthew 16:16). And then, after Jesus warned them not to tell anyone who He was, we read these words in Matthew 16:21-23:

> *"From that time Jesus began to show his disciples that he must go to Jerusalem and suffer many things from the elders and chief priests and scribes, and be killed, and on the third day be raised. And Peter took him aside and began to rebuke him, saying, 'Far be it from you, Lord! This shall never happen to you.' But he turned and said to Peter, 'Get behind me, Satan! You are a hindrance to me. For you are not setting your mind on the things of God, but on the things of man.'"*

There's a real sense in which the Bible is all about this theme—the "things of God" versus "the things of men." God goes one way—the way of holiness and righteousness, and men go another way—their "natural" way of idolatry and sin. As Augustine put it in the fourth century, it's the "City of God" pitted against the "City of Man." Remember Jesus's words of Matthew 7:13: *"Enter by the narrow gate. For the gate is wide and the way is easy that leads to destruction, and those who enter by it are many."* The narrow gate is God's way and the broad gate is man's.

Throughout the Bible God's gracious and narrow way contrasts with man's broad and destructive way. Peter, bless his heart, was leaning on—trusting in—his own understanding in saying the things he did. He was not trusting what his Lord and Master—Jesus—was telling him. So, what does it really mean to lean on one's own understanding?

Think of the most egregious and notable example of failing to trust God and leaning instead on one's own understanding. Perhaps it would be Judas Iscariot or Ananias and Sapphira (Acts 5:1-11). For me, it would have to be the abject failure of most of those whom God brought out of Egypt by His mighty hand. The Exodus ranks, in my mind, as the third most glorious display of the mighty power and sovereignty of God in all of redemptive history. And yet the Israelites quickly forgot his mighty works and returned to their *"own understanding"* of the circumstances they encountered.

The Israelites were in Egyptian slavery and completely powerless to do anything about their situation. But God wasn't powerless. Yahweh remembered the promise He had made to Abram over 400 years before, (Genesis 15:18-21), and saw the difficulties in which Abram's descendants labored. God then took the initiative. With Moses and Aaron as His representatives, God set in motion a series of spectacular plagues that ultimately led to the destruction of every first–born son of the Egyptians. Pharaoh finally allowed the Hebrew slaves to leave the country. But Pharaoh was a sore loser. He followed after the hundreds of thousands of former slaves fleeing to the banks of the Red Sea. There, Yahweh performed an incredibly great miracle. As Pharaoh and his troops approached, God opened the sea and the people walked through as if on dry ground, *"...the waters being a wall to them on their right hand and on their left."* (Exodus 14:29).

You know the rest of the story. As Pharaoh chased after the Hebrews the walls of water collapsed and Pharaoh and his entire command perished in the sea. The Hebrews were safe. They had been emancipated by God's mighty hand and sovereign will, and stood as free men and women. They were then miraculously led by a pillar of cloud by day and fire by night—the testimony of Yahweh's presence among them. And yet, almost as soon as the Israelites had their freedom, they began to complain. There wasn't enough water. There wasn't enough good food. So Yahweh had Moses strike a rock and water flowed out. God opened up the heavens and the manna flowed down for the people to eat. Still they complained. Yahweh graciously gave them instructions as to how they were to live in the Land to which He was taking them. They were to be different than the nations they would displace. By following Yahweh's Law, they were to live in harmony and fulfillment—joyfully partaking of the feast that their God had in store for them.

But, no. They had just been eyewitnesses of the most incredible event in the history of the world—the parting of the Red Sea. They were being watered and fed by very powerful miracles, but still they moaned and complained and even wanted to return to slavery. They had a gracious God who would lead them into green pastures and still waters, renew their souls, and cause them to walk in paths of righteousness and provide a free and bounteous home for them. But still they complained and murmured against their Emancipator. Yahweh showed extraordinary patience with his wayward people. But His patience would one day end. One day, the Israelites camped at a place called Kadesh in the desert of Paran. Yahweh ordered that spies be sent into the Land that He had promised to Abram and his descendants (See Numbers 13).

The twelve spies came back with reports of the incredible bounty of the land. They brought back marvelous examples of the country's fruit and vegetables. But unfortunately, ten of the spies told fearful stories of the giants who resided there. They said it would be impossible to conquer such a people. *"We are not able to go up against the people, for they are stronger than we are"* (Numbers 13:31b). Can you imagine? They had just seen the power of Yahweh exhibited in miracle upon miracle—deliverance after deliverance—and still they leaned instead on their own understanding! Only Caleb and Joshua trusted in the LORD with all of their hearts and proposed that they attack.

The people then began to cry out even more, grumbling against the LORD and against His chosen leaders, Moses and Aaron: *"Why is the LORD bringing us into this land, to fall by the sword? Our wives and our little ones will become a prey. Would it not be better for us to go back to Egypt?"* (Numbers 14:3). That was the last straw. The very idea that the people would prefer slavery in Egypt to trusting in the LORD brought ultimate calamity. Yahweh swore that the ten reluctant spies and all of those who were afraid to go into the Land would never see the Promised Land. They would all die in the desert. Of the spies, only Joshua and Caleb would see the Land that had been promised to Abraham and his descendants.

We may be tempted to look down on the treason of these backsliding Israelites who refused to enter God's rest. We may say, "If it had been me, I would have followed Caleb and Joshua!" But I have news for you. The Israelites who fell in the desert are a picture of you and me as well as a warning for us. As the writer to the Hebrews says in 4:11, *"Let us therefore strive to enter that rest, so that no one may fall by the same sort of disobedience."*

You may remember that I said earlier, "The Exodus ranks as the third most glorious display of the mighty power and sovereignty of God in all of redemptive history." What is the first? The second? Even though the Israelites had seen that absolutely certain miraculous evidence that their God was almighty and loved them completely, they didn't have the certain evidence that we have. The most awesome event in the history of the world is, of course, the birth, life, death, and resurrection of our Lord Jesus Christ—the Word made flesh.

God sent His only begotten Son into the world that His people might be freed from the bondage of Satan—pictured by the Pharaoh of old. Through the miraculous healing power of the Holy Spirit, you and I are brought out of the darkness of "Egypt"—out of the land of sin and death—and into Christ's glorious light—and ultimately, His new heavens and new earth. And yet, while we trust Him for eternal rest and peace, do we trust Him for peace and rest in the here and now? Or are we like the Israelites in the desert, sinfully complaining and longing for a return to slavery?

So, what's the second most glorious display of the mighty power and sovereignty of God in redemptive history? I believe it is God's holy Word—the Bible. Written over thousands of years by numerous authors inspired by God's Spirit. God's Word is a supernatural book whereby the God of the Exodus speaks directly to us, His people. Will we trust the promises of our loving God to us? Will we obey Him, trusting that His guidance for our lives results in His rest in the present day, when world peace is threatened by so many financial and international difficulties? Will we trust that Christ—our High King in heaven—is right now ruling over every detail and event in His universe? Or will we lean unto our own understanding and imagine a god who has created the world but who is now worrying about how events on earth will all turn out? We may even erroneously believe God can be frustrated. It's a way of thinking that is directly connected to who we are, sinners saved only by God's grace, joined to Him by simple, child-like faith in Christ's work. Augustine said it like this: We are *"simul just et peccator"*— at the same time, we are both justified and sinners. Our sin nature can lead us to walk by sight and not by faith; to walk in the understanding of own imaginations. But we must walk by faith in God's Word. Our greatest need is to listen to God.

The Doctrine of Human Depravity

"The heart is deceitful above all things, and desperately sick; who can understand it?" (Jeremiah 17:9).

I'm convinced that the most significant error most evangelical Christians make in our own *"understanding"* is in the biblical doctrine of human depravity. The understanding of depravity is crucial to our proper comprehension of what our Savior has done for us. The Bible is full not only of examples of human depravity, such as the Israelites in the desert, but of much explicit teaching regarding the doctrine. But too often, we are content to lean on our own understanding and conclude that people are basically good. Our sinfulness makes us prone to walk by sight and not by faith.

Let me give you just a few verses from the lips of Jesus. (I've provided a list of Bible verses that teach human depravity in Appendix A, since I believe this doctrine is so crucial to a proper understanding of the Christian life). In Luke 18:18-19 *"And a ruler asked him, "Good Teacher, what must I do to inherit eternal life?" And Jesus said to him, "Why do you call me good? No one is good except God alone."* And in Matthew 7:11, the Lord Jesus actually called His disciples "evil!" (Not a very politically correct way to win friends!) Here's what the Apostle Paul has to say about who we really are, quoting the Psalms and the prophet Isaiah in

Romans 3:10-18:

> "...as it is written: 'None is righteous, no, not one; no one understands; no one seeks for God. All have turned aside; together they have become worthless; no one does good, not even one.' 'Their throat is an open grave; they use their tongues to deceive.' 'The venom of asps is under their lips.' 'Their mouth is full of curses and bitterness.' 'Their feet are swift to shed blood; in their paths are ruin and misery, and the way of peace they have not known.' 'There is no fear of God before their eyes.'"

Paul is not talking about some aliens from outer space. Paul's not speaking of some race of men who have died out. He's speaking of you and me. We who have been saved by God's grace still retain that sin nature. We're not as sinful as we could be, that's true. But as a friend of mine likes to say, "We aren't as bad as we could be, because we can't commit murder or rape and still be president of the Rotary club." In other words, most of us humans understand that if we are to get along in the world and not be thrown into the slammer, or shunned from proper society, or afraid to lose our jobs or friends, we need to follow the rules of the game. We need to get along with others, not cheating them or stealing from them. We help the poor, and put on charity balls, but from what motivation? Ultimately, we do these "good" things to elevate ourselves in the eyes of others. We don't do these things for God's glory, but for our own glory! Each of us Christians is a volcano ready to erupt, but over whose cauldron the Holy Spirit has placed a cap. Only through the Spirit's restraint of sin can the world survive even the next twenty–four hours.

Sin, any sin, is cosmic rebellion against a holy God. Every sin, even the most minute peccadillo like a tiny white lie or an evil thought is worthy of eternal death. But we don't just commit one little sin. Our entire lives are filled with sin! The most despicable sin is to reject the free offer of salvation through Jesus Christ's atoning work. People everywhere do that every hour of every day. We are great sinners! And yet, we have a great Savior. No sin is too gross that God cannot forgive it through Jesus's person and work. What happened? Why is the world like it is? Remember these words in Genesis 1:26-27? *"Then God said, 'Let us make man in our image, after our likeness. And let them have dominion over the fish of the sea and over the birds of the heavens and over the livestock and over all the earth and over every creeping thing that creeps on the earth.'"*

God created mankind in His own image, in holiness and righteousness, with perfect physical and mental capabilities. But in the Fall, Adam sinned and immediately part of God's image in him was greatly tarnished and another part was totally annihilated. The part of God's image that became disjointed or distorted we might call the "material" part. Whereas in innocence, Adam had the ability to speak lovingly and to reason rightly and to live without dying, sin brought a lying tongue, rationalization, and physical death. The part of God's image that was absolutely destroyed was the spiritual part. Men and women became spiritually *"dead in trespasses and sins"* (Ephesians 2:1). Immediately after their sin, the first couple hid from God. The Creator who had been their friend was now their bitter enemy. Ever since, every man and woman—except Jesus—has been born with this same material brokenness and spiritual deadness. Every person except Jesus has been born blind to spiritual truth in a darkened world. We read these words from 2 Corinthians 4:4: *"In their case the god of this world [Satan] has blinded the minds of the unbelievers, to keep them from seeing the light of the gospel of the glory of Christ, who is the image of God."*

Jesus's mission was to restore God's image in mankind. We who have received the new birth and who trust Christ as Lord and Savior are having the spiritual and material images renewed in us, although we continue to bear the sin nature and to carry around *"this body of death"* (Romans 7:24). We also have to await the complete restoration of God's image when Christ comes for His own at the final trumpet. Meanwhile, we press on to be guided and directed by God's Word and Spirit into maturity. The goal of Christian maturity is to be conformed to the image of our Creator and Redeemer—Jesus Christ our Lord (Romans 8:29).

Not surprisingly, however, we often hear that most evangelical Protestants believe that people are basically "good." Here's a quote from *The Christian Post* on December 17, 2010:

> "The majority of Protestants and evangelicals believe that good people and people of other religions can go to heaven, according to author

> David Campbell. Campbell, who co-wrote *American Grace, How Religion Divides and Unites Us*, contends that surveys of 3,000 Americans, used to write the book, show that American people of faith, though devout, are very tolerant. So much so that most believers also believe that good people, despite their religious affiliation, can go to heaven."

Now, we may debate the accuracy of Mr. Campbell's numbers, but if even ten-percent of evangelical Christians believe that people are basically good, even good enough to be saved apart from Christ, we should be very concerned. It shows an absolute lack of biblical knowledge, and particularly, a gross misunderstanding of the Gospel.

If we are essentially good people, then why do we need the Cross of Christ? Good people only need a little-bitty savior, perhaps only themselves, while evil people need a great Savior who went to an infinite and cosmically horrible death to save them from themselves. Can you see how the work of Christ on our behalf is minimized if people are "good enough" to go to heaven based on their own good works? Do you see how God's perfect law is minimized, even rejected? Of course, we can understand why some Christians come to this conclusion. If we judge ourselves against other people, we will naturally paint ourselves with a brush dipped in self-righteousness, which is purely an indication of our total depravity. We will usually come out looking pretty good if we compare ourselves to the murderers and thieves on the local television news or in the morning newspaper. In other words, we walk by sight and not by faith, as opposed to Paul's command in 2 Corinthians 5:7.

But God's "goodness" is infinite, (Chapter 3), and He judges only on that scale. Only through trusting in the finished work of the Lord Jesus Christ can anyone be saved. In John 6:28-29, Jesus spoke to a crowd of people in Capernaum. *"Then they said to him, "What must we do, to be doing the works of God?" Jesus answered them, "This is the work of God, that you believe in him whom he has sent."* And in John 14:6: *"I am the way, and the truth, and the life. No one comes to the Father except through me."* That's the Gospel, and it's the only way to become a friend of God rather than His natural enemy (see James 4:4, for instance). Understanding human depravity is essential to understanding the Gospel, and indeed, understanding the entire Bible.

I recall that during the first several years of my Christian walk I could never explain the simple Gospel. I couldn't remember it! But when I began later to understand and believe the doctrine of human depravity—the spiritual death of every man woman and child since the Fall of Adam in the Garden of Eden, it became very memorable.

Human depravity, or as sometimes termed "original sin," is the reason Jesus had to be born of a virgin through the power of the Holy Spirit. He is the only person ever born into this world without the disabling, disjointing disease called human sin. We all otherwise have it, and we need a great Savior because of it. We have as much chance of saving ourselves as a snowball has in the middle of summer in the Sahara desert.

Perhaps the best illustration I've ever heard for why we are blind to the doctrine of human sinfulness is that of an iceberg. Ship captains understand that only ten percent of an iceberg's mass lies above the surface of the water. So, on spotting an iceberg, they give it a wide berth and steer their ship according to their larger understanding. In the same way, even we Christians can see only a small percentage of the sin that's within us. Paul understood this truth when he wrote 1 Corinthians 4:2-4:

> *"Moreover, it is required of stewards that they be found faithful. But with me it is a very small thing that I should be judged by you or by any human court. In fact, I do not even judge myself. For I am not aware of anything against myself, but I am not thereby acquitted. It is the Lord who judges me."*

In the same way, we cannot see the depths of the sinfulness within our hearts. The vast majority of our sin is hidden from us. In one respect that is a good thing. If we were to see ourselves as we truly are, we couldn't stand in the face of it. But we must be careful not to deceive ourselves into believing we are "good" people. We must walk by what the Bible says about us and not what we ourselves perceive. Brothers and sisters, this is so crucial! Don't miss it.

By the way, I've added an appendix that reiterates many of the Bible passages that teach man's depravity. If you can take some time and let those verses wash over you, the time will be well spent. Understanding that we, in our natural state, are truly *"dead in transgressions and sins"* (Ephesians 2:1), will give you a greater appreciation for what God has done for us in Jesus Christ. We have a great Savior who while we were His ungodly, sinful, enemies (Romans 5:6-10), Christ died for us. This will explain why the Reformers of the 16th century insisted that regeneration, or the new birth, logically preceeds faith and repentance in the order of salvation. In fact, it's not just the Presbyterians and other Reformed denominations who believe this crucial doctrine. Here's a recent statement from the Southern Baptist Convention, the largest evangelical denomination in America:

> "Regeneration, or the new birth, is a work of God's grace whereby believers become new creatures in Christ Jesus. It is a change of heart wrought by the Holy Spirit through conviction of sin, to which the sinner responds in repentance toward God and faith in the Lord Jesus Christ. Repentance and faith are inseparable experiences of grace" (www.sbc.net, Baptist Faith and Message, 2000, IV, Salvation).

The irresistible conclusion to this statement is that it is God who chooses sinners to be saved. Spiritually dead people will not choose God. They are dead. This doctrine also invites the inevitable conclusion that God is absolutely sovereign—His will cannot be thwarted. He reigns supreme over every event, including the salvation of sinners.

The Bible states most clearly that every person's ultimate default location is eternal separation from the love and grace of God—Hell. Of all the words in the Bible regarding this place of darkness and disintegration, by far the most are spoken by Jesus. For instance, in Mark 9:43 He says, *"And if your hand causes you to sin, cut it off. It is better for you to enter life crippled than with two hands to go to hell, to the unquenchable fire."* Merely ask yourself, "If I'm basically a good person, why should God submit me to everlasting condemnation?"

I hope you'll arrive at the conclusion, "Well, maybe I'm not such a good person after all." If we were "good" people, God would be unjust in sending us to Hell, wouldn't He? But God is altogether just so that's not possible. So, what if God chooses to save some people? Is that injustice on God's part? Of course not. God is not required to save anyone. But He does save some. Remember these well known verses from John 3:16-18. Note particularly the words "condemned already" in verse 18:

> *"For God so loved the world, that he gave his only Son, that whoever believes in him should not perish but have eternal life. For God did not send his Son into the world to condemn the world, but in order that the world might be saved through him. Whoever believes in him is not condemned, but whoever does not believe is condemned already, because he has not believed in the name of the only Son of God."*

A person who is *"condemned already"* is not a "good" person. Condemnation is justified in God's eyes only for evil people, spiritually *"dead in trespasses and sins."*

People as Coiled Springs

A good way to look at the world is this: **All** truly good things come from God. **Only** truly good things come from God. As a function of His goodness, God's Spirit is controlling sin in the world by His awesome power. Imagine people as compressed coiled springs ready to spring up and commit sin. Now imagine a large supernatural hand pressing down upon all these coiled springs in the world. It's the Holy Spirit's "hand" so to speak, which depresses sin and encourages righteousness. Evil occurs when God's Spirit takes His hand back a little and people's springs—their hearts—are allowed to do what is foremost in them—to commit sin. So God isn't the author of sin, but in His secret will He allows sin and uses it for His Holy purposes. Think of Pharaoh whose heart was "hardened" by God (Exodus 4:21, for instance). Yahweh merely took His "hand" off the "spring" of Pharaoh's heart and sin sprang forth. Pharaoh just did what the natural inclination of his sinful heart dictated.

This is difficult news for us "good" people. When we compare ourselves with others we feel reasonably righteous. But the Bible says that the plumb line or standard of righteousness isn't other sinners, it is God Himself. And God has sent us His perfect Law and His perfect Man to show us to whom we must compare ourselves. In doing so, we either see that we fail miserably and seek God's mercy, or we thumb our noses at God and trust in our own understanding. We must walk by faith in God's Word and not by sight.

Faith and Instrument Flight Rules

When I was in the US Army many years ago, I was stationed in southern Germany for two years. Occasionally I would be required to travel to Rhine–Main Air Base in Frankfurt, about 100 miles from my base. Our battle group had a wing of perhaps 10 helicopters. All I needed to do was phone the staff of that helicopter wing and they would gladly give me a lift. They always agreed because they could use their time in the air to practice Instrument Flight Rules (IFR). That means that the pilot would place a big metal or plastic hood over his head so that all he could see was the instrument panel. He was neither allowed to look at visual clues outside the aircraft, nor respond to what his body was telling him about the attitude and navigation of his helicopter. He had to trust solely in what the instruments were telling him, and not be swayed by trusting in the "seat of his pants" which can lie to him. In the same way, we are to be guided by God's Word and not by our own corrupt understanding. We are to walk by faith in what God says in His Word and not and not by our own understanding.

We'll make several stops while looking at trusting our own understanding versus trusting God for all things. First, we'll look at idolatry—the disobedience of the first and second commandments. We'll see how idols of our hearts focus and excite patterns of sin in us, so that we break the rest of God's commandments. We'll look also at some tributaries of idolatry, such as the notion of chance or luck, as well as legalism, the most insidious form of idolatry. Then we'll take up the subjects of human presuppositions and traditions that skew our understanding of the truth of God's Word. Finally in this section, we'll discuss how secular world-views cause even committed Christians to walk in functional atheism—"red light" atheism.

Here's Our Big Problem: Idolatry

John Calvin was a 16th century theologian and one of the foremost leaders in the Reformation. Among his many works, which include commentaries on some forty–nine books of the Bible is his magnum opus—Calvin's *Institutes of the Christian Religion*. Here's what Calvin says on the topic of idolatry. Calvin refers to Genesis 39:19 when Rachel steals her father Laban's household gods. Calvin says, "Hence we may infer, that the human mind is, so to speak, a perpetual forge of idols." Then a few sentences later, "And daily experience shows, that the flesh is always restless until it has obtained some figment like itself, with which it may vainly solace itself as a representation of God" (Both quotes from Book I, XI, 8). In other words, Calvin says that the human mind wants to manufacture ideas and created things in which it can trust as opposed to trusting in the living God.

But you argue, "Wait, Beasley, I don't forge idols of metal or carve them of wood to represent God! That's so Old Testament! That's so ancient!" That's true, and neither do I make statues to worship. But that doesn't mean that idolatry is dead in the 21st century. We've just become much more sophisticated in our idolatry. Instead of worshiping and serving gods and goddesses like Baal, Dagon, Ashtoreth, and Diana of the Ephesians, we worship false gods like Power, Sex, Money, Pleasure, a Wife or Husband, Comfort, Beauty, Education, Career, Security, Peace and Quiet, and the like. We're not so much different from the Baal worshipers of Elijah's day. We want exactly the same things. We just skip the middleman—the carved or forged image.

Even we Christians look to things other than God for our "solace" as Calvin says—our comfort and security. The Apostle Paul said it like this in Romans 1:25: *"...they exchanged the truth about God for a lie and worshiped and served the creature rather than the Creator, who is blessed forever! Amen."* We humans will create our own gods in which we place the trust that only our heavenly Father deserves. Left to ourselves, we worship and serve the creature rather than the Creator.

Let's go way back in the Old Testament and look at Exodus 20:1-6:

> *"And God spoke all these words, saying, 'I am the LORD your God, who brought you out of the land of Egypt, out of the house of slavery. "You shall have no other gods before me. "You shall not make for yourself a carved image, or any likeness of anything that is in heaven above, or that is in the earth beneath, or that is in the water under the earth. You shall not bow down to them or serve them, for I the LORD your God am a jealous God, visiting the iniquity of the fathers on the children to the third and the fourth generation of those who hate me, but showing steadfast love to thousands of those who love me and keep my commandments.'"*

Notice first that the Ten Commandments begin with God announcing that He is a gracious and merciful God—the God who acts on behalf of His people, even though they are a treacherous and treasonous people. He has, by His almighty power and sovereign will brought His people, Israel, out of slavery in Egypt. As we've mentioned, although a historical fact, the Exodus becomes for us today a metaphor for the historical fact of the Cross. It refers to how God by His great power and sovereign will brings us out of slavery to Satan and into the ultimate *"Promised Land"*—*"the new heavens and the new earth"* (Isaiah 65:17; 2 Peter 3:13).

The first commandment—*"You shall have no other gods before me,"* means simply and in the context of our study, *"Trust in the LORD with all your heart"*—Proverbs 3:5a. The second commandment says, *"You shall not make for yourself a carved image. . ."* In effect it is commanding, *"And do not lean on your own understanding"*—Proverbs 3:5b. To trust in our own understanding always means that we will trust in some created thing rather than our Creator God. We will worship and serve finite creaturely things other than the immortal, infinite God who controls all events. We will attribute the power and the glory that only the LORD deserves, to someone or something else. We will make as our true and ultimate source of security, comfort, and pleasure someone or something apart from the one, true God. That is what idolatry is.

My wife, Amy's mother grew up near Providence, Rhode Island. I would wager that if one walked down the street in that city and asked ten passers–by what "providence" means, only a few would know. We've basically lost that word's meaning from our vocabulary. The Latin roots of the word providence are *"pro,"* which means, "before," and *"video,"* which means "to see." The word originally spoke of the God who "sees before." Remember the words of Jesus in Matthew 6:31-32: *"Therefore do not be anxious, saying, 'What shall we eat?' or 'What shall we drink?' or 'What shall we wear?' For the Gentiles seek after all these things, and **your heavenly Father knows that you need them all**."* God knows our needs even before they arise in us. Not only that, He also provides us with everything we need for today, and into eternity. He is the God of providence. Only the true God *"...will supply every need of yours according to his riches in glory in Christ Jesus"* (Philippians 4:19). The problem is that we don't believe God will supply all of our needs or wants. So, in unbelief, we turn to idols to have our needs, our desires and wants, met. In doing so, we lean on our own understanding.

So, idolatry is simply trusting some created thing other than the God who created the universe and who flung the stars into space. Idolatry is not the reason we sin. We sin because we're sinners cursed from the Fall. But idolatry is the reason we commit the kind of sins that we commit. We might say that idolatry shapes our sin life. Idolatry is at the foundation, the inception of every little peccadillo, every lie, every infraction of God's law. One might ask, "Why is the command not to have other gods the first commandment?" It's because all other sins flow from disobedience to this first commandment. Idolatry is the wisdom of the world as opposed to the wisdom of God. It is attempting to build one's identity and self-worth on anything but the God of the Bible. Idolatry is taking a good thing and making it an ultimate thing, a thing in which one places his or her trust for comfort and security. As we've said, anything qualifies as an idol: Money, power, career, looks, comfort, talents, relationships, control, parents, government, children. . . anything, even good things. This is what idols do: They promise life and satisfaction, but they bring disintegration, isolation, and ultimately eternal death. Only the living God, through His Gospel of grace, can deliver on His promises, bringing satisfaction, wholeness, and abundant life. (By the way, I am indebted to pastor Tim Keller and his book, "Counterfeit Gods," for some of the ideas expressed here. It is a book I highly recommend for further study of these issues.)

Some Examples of Idolatry From Scripture

Adam and Eve

One doesn't have to turn very far in the Bible to see idolatry raise its ugly head. Our first parents decided to trust in the word of the Serpent, the creature, rather than in the Word of their Creator. They were attracted by a false god and that attraction produced sin. We read in Genesis 3:6: *"So when the woman saw that the tree was good for food, and that it was a delight to the eyes, and that the tree was to be desired to make one wise, she took of its fruit and ate, and she also gave some to her husband who was with her, and he ate."* Notice that the forbidden fruit was appealing to the lust of the eyes, the lust of the flesh, and the pride of life. But the eating of it had been forbidden by their Friend—the Creator God—with whom the first couple had walked in close fellowship. Their disobedience was an incredibly irrational act. There was no prior cause for it apart from a conscious, voluntary, sinful response to the Serpent's leading. A mysterious change came upon Adam and Eve that was not forced upon them, neither compelled by the Serpent nor by their wonderful environment in the Garden. It was not made inevitable by something within their God-created constitutions.

Adam and Eve were given completely free wills, both to choose for the good or for evil, what we might call "the power of contrary choice." But nothing in their makeup as God's creatures caused them to lean toward evil. In fact, it was just the opposite. Genesis 1:31 says of Adam and all creation, *"And God saw everything that he had made, and behold, it was very good."* Made in God's own image, the man and the woman were very good and beloved by their Creator. He created Adam and Eve in righteousness, not in the grips of evil, as their fallen descendants would be. But in a way that is beyond our discovery or understanding, they contradicted their innate disposition to love God and serve and obey Him. Instead, they sought meaning and fulfillment in disobedience to their Creator's command and warnings.

What was the idol that Adam and Eve sought after? I believe they sought the idols of freedom and personal autonomy. The first couple sought freedom from their Creator, and the ability to be a law unto themselves. I believe that for better or for worse, without God's leadership we will always choose in the direction that we perceive to be in our own selfish interests. Therefore, I believe that Adam and Eve thought in that moment of decision, that their own self-interests were best served by listening to the Serpent. They wanted freedom and they wanted to be a law unto themselves. They wanted selfish, absolute control over their lives and future.

Their decision to turn their backs on a perfect life of peace and fulfillment in the Garden of Eden was irrational, absurd, outrageous, unimaginable, unthinkable—lunacy! But by that one decision, the world was plunged into darkness and utmost tragedy. Instead of freedom came bondage. Instead of life came death. Instead of autonomy came slavery to Satan and idolatry and a sin nature. Instead of love came hatred, murder, and every evil. Instead of peace came violence and war. Instead of real life came real death. The first couple lost the freedom and sanctitude of friendship with their Creator and put the created order under an unimaginable, torturous curse. Adam and Eve also lost for themselves and their descendants the power of contrary choice. From that moment onward, humans would make selfish, evil choices. They had died to the good. They became spiritually dead in trespasses and sin.

Paul says it best about the first couple and their offspring in Romans 1:21-22: *"For although they knew God, they did not honor him as God or give thanks to him, but they became futile in their thinking, and their foolish hearts were darkened. Claiming to be wise, they became fools..."* This statement is true of the first couple and their descendants ever since. Verse 23 continues: *"...exchanged the glory of the immortal God for images resembling mortal man and birds and animals and creeping things."* And then, summing up his arguments for mankind's depravity, Paul says in Romans 1:25: *"...they exchanged the truth about God for a lie and worshiped and served the creature rather than the Creator, who is blessed forever! Amen."*

Ever since the Fall, the first couple's descendants have struggled to make sense of life. Like Adam and Eve we naturally hide from God (Genesis 3:8). Left to our sinful selves, apart from the Spirit's work in regeneration, we don't want anything to do with the one true God. We believe freedom and fulfillment will be found in things other than God. We don't even care to understand that true freedom and fulfillment come only from running to God and not away from Him. We humans, in our innate sinfulness, long for the Garden of Eden. But we want to return to a garden without God. So, we turn to godlike things. In ancient days, people turned to idols that pointed to supposed supernatural gods and goddesses. Today, we worship more material gods like power, money, and sex. As we've said before, we've just replaced the "middlemen"—carved or forged statues—with the real, underlying "lords" that are supposed to make us happy.

I used to have an occasional problem sometimes while walking down stairs. My right ankle would pop out of place. It would become dislocated, as it were. It was painful, and I couldn't walk until it slid back into its proper position. The Fall produced in all people a dislocation of another sort. Keller quotes Dorothy

Sayers who said sin is a "deep, interior dislocation of the soul." Instead of walking in the Garden in full friendship with our Creator, in unbelief we now want nothing to do with Him. The image of God, given to humans in the beginning, is still there but it has become radically distorted in a material or broad sense, and annihilated in a spiritual sense.

Adam's Son Cain

It wasn't long before the first couple's sin began to spread to their immediate family. Cain murdered his brother Abel (See Genesis 4:1-16). Why? Why did Cain murder Abel? The writer to the Hebrews says this in 11:4: *"By faith Abel offered to God a more acceptable sacrifice than Cain, through which he was commended as righteous..."*

Matthew Henry comments:

> "Abel brought a sacrifice of atonement from the first-lings of the flock, acknowledging himself a sinner who deserved to die, and only hoping for mercy through the great Sacrifice. Cain's proud rage and enmity against the accepted worshiper of God, led to the awful effects the same principles have produced in every age; the cruel persecution, and even murder of believers" *(Matthew Henry's Commentary on Genesis 4:8-14).*

Cain was angry at God. The Creator was his arch-enemy. Can we pinpoint it? Why was Cain angry? What sin was crouching at his door? What did Cain truly worship?

I believe that Cain pridefully worshiped himself. He refused to worship God by faith through a bloody sacrifice, and instead brought the work of his own hands. He trusted his own way versus God's command. His idolatry led to conflict and in foolish pride and jealousy, and he murdered his brother in an attempt at self–justification and self–elevation.

This is the story of redemptive history. You have probably noticed that the Bible is full of conflict. It's all about the one true God versus a host of gods or idols of human imagination and manufacture. We see either idolatry or the effects of idolatry on just about every page of holy Scripture. The only hope we have to escape from its dead-end street is the Gospel of Jesus Christ. He only is *"the way and the truth and the life"* (John 14:6). Only Christ can break us free from the bondage of idolatry and death.

The Babel Builders

In Genesis 11:4 we read, *"Then they said, 'Come, let us build ourselves a city and a tower with its top in the heavens, and let us make a name for ourselves, lest we be dispersed over the face of the whole earth.'"* We're told specifically in this verse why the tower of Babel was built. It was to *"make a name"* for its builders. Pride. Self aggrandizement. Self promotion. Selfishness. The men of Babel wanted to get from beneath their Creator's watchful eye and live their lives dependent only upon themselves. They wanted to be like God, elevated to His realm of authority. They soon discovered that God will not put up with such foolishness. He confused their language and scattered them over the face of the earth (Genesis 11:9).

Jacob, Rachel, and Leah

In his little volume, *Counterfeit Gods*, Pastor Keller goes into great detail about the idolatries of Jacob, Leah, and Rachel in Genesis 29 through 31. Let's just look at only one verse that he discusses: *"When Rachel saw that she bore Jacob no children, she envied her sister. She said to Jacob, "Give me children, or I shall die!"'* (Genesis 30:1). In that day and age, for a married woman to remain barren was a serious matter—a tragedy—both culturally and economically. Rachel was barren and it was her ruination. She was ready to commit suicide! Notice she's blaming Jacob for her barrenness. She's not hoping in her Creator, but in God's creature, a child. (Her display of anger at Jacob is a clear indication of her idolatry, as we'll see later.) This is the epitome of idolatry, wanting something so desperately that, even though it may be a good thing, it becomes an ultimate thing in one's life. Of course, in Genesis 30:22-23, we see that Rachel turns from idolatry and places her trust in God to provide her with a son: *"Then God remembered Rachel, and God listened to her and opened her womb. She conceived and bore a son and said, "God has taken away my reproach."'* Her son, of course, was Joseph.

Herod the Great and Other Kings

We can find examples of extreme idolatry in every king or ruler in Scripture. We need only think of the Pharaoh in Exodus who blatantly refused to acknowledge

Yahweh, trusting instead in the gods of Egypt. (He must have thought that since Yahweh's people were in slavery, and Egypt's people were free, Egypt's gods were by far the strongest!) Saul was Yahweh's choice as the first king of Israel. But power and riches got to Saul's heart and he forsook the one true God to follow after his own desires. Even king David succumbed to idols. In one moment of his life, David wanted Bathsheba more than he wanted to follow Yahweh and it brought him trouble all the rest of his days.

In the New Testament, we have, among others, the example of Herod the Great. You will recall how in Matthew 2, the wise men visit Herod and speak to him about the child who was to be born King of the Jews. Herod greeted the news with anxiety. Was this child to take his power from him? He told the wise men to bring him news of the baby, but, of course, by God's hand, they returned to their land by another route than through Jerusalem. Later, Herod's idol of power would lead to anger and murder, as he forced the execution of all male children two years old and younger in the area around Bethlehem. Herod the Great was a control freak who was powerful and successful, and who delighted in his rebellion against God. He built a marvelous Temple to show the people what a good, religious guy he was. But inside, Herod was full of pride, anger, and hostility toward God, trusting instead in his own abilities while serving his idol of power.

Herod is an example, like all of us who trust in our own understanding, of the cosmic spiritual warfare being raged since the Fall. It's the hostility between Satan's seed and *"the seed of the woman"* (Genesis 3:15). As James says in James 4:1-2: *"What causes quarrels and what causes fights among you? Is it not this, that your passions are at war within you? You desire and do not have, so you murder. You covet and cannot obtain, so you fight and quarrel. You do not have, because you do not ask."* Idolatry is at the root of much that is wrong with America and the world. Personal battles and major wars almost always have their beginnings in the worship of conflicting idols.

Ancient Idolatry

While modern day idols are more difficult to identify in a person, idolatry among the pagan nations in the Old and New Testaments is usually easy to spot. Each ancient nation had its own gods, which supposedly ruled within the confines of national boundaries. The technical term for these national gods is "henotheism." One example of henotheism is that of the Syrian general Naaman, who being healed from his leprosy by the LORD, said this: *"...please let there be given to your servant two mule loads of earth, for from now on your servant will not offer burnt offering or sacrifice to any god but the LORD"* (2 Kings 5:17). Naaman thought that in order to worship Yahweh—the God of the Israelites—he needed to worship Him on Israeli soil. So when he returned to Syria he took a lot of Israeli dirt with him.

We also recall the Ark of the Covenant was being captured by the Philistines. We read in 1 Samuel 5:1-2: *"When the Philistines captured the ark of God, they brought it from Ebenezer to Ashdod. Then the Philistines took the ark of God and brought it into the house of Dagon and set it up beside Dagon."* Dagon was the god of the Philistines and reigned within their borders. Recall how puny Dagon looked after the beating he took from Yahweh! (1 Samuel 5:1-8) In 1 Kings 11:33, Yahweh speaks of those kings of Israel who had left His worship and had given themselves to, *"Ashtoreth the goddess of the Sidonians, Chemosh the god of the Moabites, and Milcom the god of the Ammonites."* These were all national gods, and were all opposed to the one true God. The henotheistic nations thought Yahweh was merely a god like their own, restricted to national boundaries.

Ancient pagans thought these gods were real. The reason they gave themselves to the worship of these fictitious gods was to have a semblance of control over their own lives. Like the first couple, the people of the pagan nations wanted freedom to do what they wanted to do and figured their gods could provide what they needed. So the ancient carved or forged idols merely represented the supernatural power behind them. We might say that people thought the carved or forged statue channeled the power of the god or goddess it represented. To worship Dagon or Ashtoreth or any of the false gods would be unthinkable without the carved or forged idol. These gods, then, were to respond to the worshiper's allegiance by doing what the worshipers wanted. It was what we might call a *quid pro quo*. The people thought: "I'll sacrifice to the image of Dagon and he'll bring rain for the spring crop." "I'll give my children in the fire of Molech, and he'll bring me victory over the nation next door." But Yahweh doesn't work like that.

The Creator of the universe is the God who brings victory over enemies and food to eat, but He doesn't cut deals. No one controls Yahweh. Like Aslan in C.S. Lewis's *The Lion, The Witch, and the Wardrobe*, God is "good, but He isn't safe" in the sense He alone is sovereign and He isn't controllable. God and God alone is in control. God and God alone ordains everything that happens in the future or that has ever happened in the past, and yet He is not the author of sin.

The same thing is true of modern gods. "I'll work in this job for forty years, and its pension will keep me in my old age." "I'll devote myself to my spouse and he will never leave me." "I'll put 10% of my earnings in the stock market each month, and I'll have plenty later on." Now, there's nothing wrong with devotion, working, or saving with the future in mind. In fact, they are really good things. But to place one's complete trust in these things, as many have, is only to discover deep disappointment in the end. The same is true of any created things: the government, children, education, and myriad other things that we are drawn to for safety. Only the true God is safe. He is "safe" in the sense that all who put their ultimate trust in Him will never be disappointed. As Romans 8:28 so aptly says, *"And we know that for those who love God all things work together for good, for those who are called according to his purpose."* God will never leave us or forsake us.

The "Family Tree" of Idolatry

I believe that idols—false gods—exist in a hierarchy, in what we might call a "family tree" of idols. Behind every idol, lurking in the background, is Satan. He is the father of lies (John 8:44), and, indeed, the father of all idolatry and sin (Genesis 3:1ff). So we put our peg way back in the Garden of Eden where we see the Serpent—the deceiver—operating. Next in line in this family tree comes "pride." Through human procreation, original sin is passed along the family tree to everyone who has ever lived, save One—our Lord Jesus—thanks to His conception in the Virgin Mary by the Holy Spirit. At the root of sin—every sin—is pride, an overweening desire to serve and elevate oneself. Pride boils down to this: Self-seeking, self-glorifying, selfishness. Since pride is father Satan's core sin, (Ezekiel 28:12-17), I see pride as the "mother" of all sins. I think it's helpful to think of Satan as the father of sin and pride as sin's mother.

Deep-seated, Far Away Idols

Next comes what Keller calls "deep" idols, also known as "soul" idols or "heart" idols. We may also call these idols "far away" idols, in that they will produce idols that are "nearby" much like the images of ancient gods represented the god behind the image who was unseen or far away. These deep-seated, often hidden idols, are those that flow from pride and become ultimate objects of trust and hope for the depraved mind. These are idols that if debunked, destroyed, or removed, their loss will ruin the one who trusted in them, such as Rachel was devastated when she said she would rather die than be childless. He or she will have no reason to live, because they've built their whole foundation of life upon an idol. These idols include things like beauty, power, personal honor, love, and the like. Desire for these things may be encouraged by the culture, one's religion, the government, or any other aspect of society may elevate these qualities to god-like stature. The idolater seeks to replace God with one of these idols as the central reason to live and the foundation of his or her self-worth and personal identity. So "far away" idols are those lurking in the background. They attract nearby or surface idols, those idols that may be seen.

Nearby or Surface Idols

Next along my family tree of idolatry is what could be called a "nearby" idol. Let's suppose the "faraway" idol in a person's life is "power." One thinks, how will I get power? What is the best way to achieve power? One might think of several paths. We think of political power. We may also think of the power that comes from wealth. Suppose our power seeker determines that his best path to power is through the accumulation of money. The creation of wealth will be his method to serve his "far away" idol of power. The accumulation of wealth, then, becomes his "nearby" idol. It is "nearby" in the sense that he can run his business or check His stocks every day to see how they are doing in serving his "far away" quest for power.

Much like his counterparts in the ancient Near East, he bows down to his "nearby" idol, but his real idol is far away, like the false supernatural entities that the ancient idolater worshiped through their metal and wood images. These far away and nearby idols then attract sin. We have seen how in Herod's life, his faraway idol of total power, worshiped by the nearby idol of his cherished position as Rome's client king, caused him to murder the children around Bethlehem, a gross violation of the sixth commandment.

In many societies, the primary idol is family pride. In these shame and honor based societies, a person who faces a shameful situation such as the loss of a job or other embarrassment, would often commit suicide, a violation of the sixth commandment. Many Japanese soldiers during World War II committed *hare-kari* rather than face surrender. If a Japanese officer lost his command, more than likely he would take his own life rather than face others. Shame or disgrace is the worst thing that can happen to a man or woman of many Asian countries. Oh, what freedom they could find in the Gospel of God's grace, which alone demolishes this and all other idols!

One thing we must keep in mind is that specific idols aren't as easily determined as I have perhaps suggested. They can be slippery. Idols can vary in intensity and abundance. They can be impossible for the idolater to pin down and very difficult for the observer to do so.

Humans as Electrons

Think of humans as tiny electrons. Like little electrons, we cannot exist on our own apart from being drawn into a compound of some sort. Hydrogen atoms do not exist in an individual state in earth's atmosphere. They are attracted and attached to either another hydrogen molecule or another element like oxygen. In that union, attached to two oxygen atoms, they become H_2O, or water. So also are we, because of the power of sin working in us, naturally drawn to some sort of idol, unless we are called by God to be attached to Himself—to Christ. Even then, idols may and will attract believers, and as 1 John 5:21 warns, we must be very wary of them.

Idols as Giant Magnets

In another sense, an idol is like a magnet, only it doesn't attract metal or other magnets—it attracts sin. Think of a magnet with positive and negative poles. A faraway idol is a magnet that draws in lesser, surface idols, and these idols attract sinful thoughts and behavior. Certainly idolatry in itself is sin, violating the first two commandments, but it is a higher and more central sin in that it attracts sinful thoughts and activities. For the unbeliever—every unbeliever—there is a faraway idols lurking. Like a magnet, it draws him or her to ultimate disillusionment and destruction. Idols can only promise life, satisfaction, and security, but they cannot truly deliver. For the Christian, there are two magnets. One is much larger and infinitely more potent than these lesser magnets of idolatry. God, in His wisdom and power intercedes for us by His Spirit, and by His mighty power and sovereign will, draws us away from the idols of our imagination. Once saved by God's grace, we are pulled into God's kingdom of righteousness. At the same time, the other idolatrous magnets in our lives continue to attract us in the opposing direction. These are the idols of which John speaks in 1 John 5:21: *"Dear children, keep yourselves from idols."*

Think of God and idols having the same polarity and humans having the opposite polarity. The equal polarities of idols and the one true God don't attract one another. In fact it is just the opposite—they are repelled one from the other. Just like when a positive pole of a magnet is placed near another magnet's positive pole, they repel each other. Dead in trespasses and sins, humans aren't attracted to the one true God unless made alive (charged) by God's Spirit. Unbelievers are attracted only to idols. Believers are also attracted to idols, except that the power of the God who calls us is infinitely greater than the attractive power of idols.

Perhaps you're wondering, "What about you, Beasley? What are the idols in your life?" Amazingly, as I have grown older in years and also grown in Christ due to the gracious power and leading of God's Spirit, my idols seem fewer and smaller. But many are still there. I now see comfort as high on the list. My far away idol is that I want an easy and comfortable life.

One of my nearby idols is the TV where I mainly watch football and basketball from my recliner. But throughout my life I've been attracted to things like wanting respect, my children, retirement, love, travel, fame, and being liked by others. None of these things are bad. But as I've grown, God has caused me to see the futility of all these things compared to His love and His ways. Oh, these old idols still surface from time to time, but I love to study God's Word and to write about His grace and wisdom. I love to worship God and to teach others about Christ and His marvelous, free salvation. But all of that is not from me at all, but only from the gracious God who has called me to love Him and to want only what He wants and that His will be done.

How Can We Recognize Idols in Our Lives?

You might ask, "But how do we know when we are trusting idols rather than trusting God?" The answer may lie in several directions. Let's look at a few:

What Do You Highly Esteem?

Idols may be seen in what a person highly reveres or holds dear. What is most highly valued in your mind? Is it your good looks? Your athletic ability? Your intellect? Your heritage? Your country? Your position in society? Another way is to ask ourselves, "What do I love excessively?" Love is an act of worship. Do you love something more than you love God? We love our wives or husbands, our mothers and fathers, but as Jesus commands in Matthew 10:37: *"Whoever loves father or mother more than me is not worthy of me, and whoever loves son or daughter more than me is not worthy of me…"* Jesus taught that loved ones can take God's place in one's life.

What are You Hoping For?

To further identify your idols, ask yourself, "In what am I placing my hope? Am I looking to my wealth? My pension? My family inheritance? My wife, husband, or children? Are you hoping in your education? Hope is an act of worship, as it places ones reliance—trust—upon a person or thing it values ultimately. God says that we are to hope in Him alone for the future. Only in Christ will our hopes be completely fulfilled.

What Do You Want More than Anything Else?

Here's one other question to ask: "What do I desire more than anything else in the world? Fame? Riches? Security? Do I want a beautiful wife or a handsome husband? Or do I desire to be like Jesus? To commune with Him? To have Him guide my life? Do I desire Him over all other things? Do I value the things of this world rather than the new world that Christ has given me as an inheritance? Am I so earthly minded that I'm no heavenly good?

What Do You Fear?

Another way is to examine our fears which always point in the direction of our hope. In other words, we fear that what we want to happen in our lives will not happen or we fear losing what we most value. We're afraid that the future holds loss and not gain. It should come as no surprise that the number one command of Christ and His apostles is "Don't be afraid." As mentioned earlier, I've counted 19 times in the New Testament that we are commanded not to be afraid. We read verses like John 14:1: *"Let not your hearts be troubled. Believe in God; believe also in me..."* And 1 Peter 3:12-14 gives us these words:

> *"For the eyes of the Lord are on the righteous, and his ears are open to their prayer. But the face of the Lord is against those who do evil. Now who is there to harm you if you are zealous for what is good? But even if you should suffer for righteousness' sake, you will be blessed. Have no fear of them, nor be troubled.'"*

We are not to fear because our loving God is in absolute control of all events. Idols may appear powerful, but in reality, any of their apparent power has only been temporarily granted by the all-powerful God. And He may take it away without warning. This does not mean that we are not to be cautious in driving or making our homes secure, but that fear is not to rule our lives.

What Do You Day-Dream About?

Another indication of an idol in your life is your answer to the question, "When I'm by myself and alone in my thoughts, what do I dream about or long for?" Maybe your thoughts go to a new car, or a better house, or a wife or husband. You tell yourself, when I get that, I'll be happy. Perhaps you are drawn to romantic or sexual fantasies. Maybe you have convinced yourself that you'll be happy when you achieve a certain title at work. You perhaps dream of fame. Many have longed for fame only to discover terrible disappointment when they achieved it. They were still the same old person they were before. Actual fame was not at all what it promised to be.

Are There Conflicts in Your Life?

Another way is to see idols in a person's life is through conflict. James 4:1-4 describes how our conflicts stem from the idols in our lives:

"What causes quarrels and what causes fights among you? Is it not this, that your passions are at war within you? You desire and do not have, so you murder. You covet and cannot obtain, so you fight and quarrel. You do not have, because you do not ask. You ask and do not receive, because you ask wrongly, to spend it on your passions. You adulterous people! Do you not know that friendship with the world is enmity with God? Therefore whoever wishes to be a friend of the world makes himself an enemy of God."

There's a real sense in which the book of James is all about trusting the creature rather than the Creator. Even though he doesn't use the words "idol" or "idolatry" in the epistle, I believe a central theme of James to be a warning about idolatry. Notice in these verses that the idol or idols in one's life may bring conflict. They may conflict with the idols of another person, say a spouse or loved one. You want to go to the beach this summer, and she wants to visit her parents. In Christ, you work it out. In unbridled idolatry, conflict reigns.

In What Do Your Principally Delight?

Similarly, ask yourself, "In what do I rejoice? If you delight in anything more than worshiping God, being in communion with Him, and seeing all things as gifts from His hand, then you are practicing idolatry. In what do you glory? Where do you find your high position? In your talents? In your intelligence? Your good looks? Your family tree? Or seek glory only in God who gives us all things freely to enjoy? One of my favorite verses in Scripture is 1 Corinthians 4:7: *"For who sees anything different in you? What do you have that you did not receive? If then you received it, why do you boast as if you did not receive it?"* We have nothing good that did not come to us from God's hand. Only He gives us life and breath and everything good (Acts 17:31).

For What Cause Are You Zealous?

Here's another idol–revealing question: "For what am I zealous?" Do you see political causes equal to or greater than the Gospel? Do you have zeal for some moral cause more than zeal for Christ's Gospel? Would you give your life for your country but not for your God? What in your life, if anything, tends to get in the way of your prayer life, your worship of the One True God? Do you stay in bed on Sunday morning rather than getting up for worship? Why?

To Whom Do You Owe Thanks?

Finally, ask yourself, "To whom or what am I grateful?" To that which we are most indebted and grateful, we worship. As Paul says in 1 Thessalonians 5:16-18, *"Rejoice always, pray without ceasing, give thanks in all circumstances; for this is the will of God in Christ Jesus for you."* We'll discuss the big secret to the Christian life in chapter 4 when we take up the subject of *"and He will make straight your paths."* The secret is in thanksgiving and contentment. Paul said in Philippians 4:11-13:

> *"..Not that I am speaking of being in need, for I have learned in whatever situation I am to be content. I know how to be brought low, and I know how to abound. In any and every circumstance, I have learned the secret of facing plenty and hunger, abundance and need. I can do all things through him who strengthens me."*

An honest Christian may ask, "I love my wife, and I would be devastated if I lost her. Is she an idol in my life?" It depends. Do you see her as a gift from God, and thank God for her? It's obvious that you would be hurt severely if she died, but would you be utterly devastated—take your own life, for instance? If it's the former, she's not an idol but a wonderful gift of God's grace for which you are thankful. If it's the latter, she is an ultimate thing that will destroy you if she's taken from you. No one or no thing can replace the living God.

But even God can become an idol. In chapter 3, we'll speak more about this problem, but it's worth mentioning here. An example from Scripture of this happening is Jesus's parable of "The Prodigal Son" (Luke 15:11-32). Most sermons seem to deal with the younger son who ran off and squandered his inheritance on wild, idolatrous living. But he finally come to his senses and returns to the waiting arms of his father. It's the other son, the older brother who has the real problem. He doesn't really want his father, he only wants what his father can give him. That can be true of us. Do we really want God? Or do we just want what God can do for us? God can become an idol, as we'll see, in more ways than one.

Dealing With Our Idols

The True God of the Bible

Only the true God of the Bible is both "nearby" and "far away." The true God is far away in that He is transcendent—He is not a part of creation as opposed to what the far eastern religions such as Buddhism believe. But God is also immanent—He is Immanuel, God with us (Matthew 1:23). Of course, God is also within His people in the person of His Spirit. Only the Christian God has this quality—to be both transcendent and immanent. The gods of the Hindus are only immanent—part of creation. The Muslim's Allah is only transcendent, as is the god in which the modern Jew worships. One thing we must keep in mind is that modern idolatry isn't as easily determined as I have perhaps suggested. It can be slippery. Idols can vary in intensity and in abundance. They can be impossible for the idolater to see, and very difficult for a mere observer to pin down.

Fearing God

Once we recognize idols in our lives, how can we deal with them? How do we get rid of the idols in our lives? One just can't will them to be gone. Something or someone needs to take their place in your heart. That someone is Jesus Christ, and that something is His Gospel of grace alone, through faith alone, in Christ alone. The one word that solves idol worship is "fear." But this is no ordinary fear. The fear I'm talking about is the fear of God. To fear Him is the way to avoid idolatry, and hence all these other fears which may plague us when we *"lean on our own understanding."* The fear of God is unlike all other fears. You may recall in Psalms 111:10, the psalmist says: *"The fear of the LORD is the beginning of wisdom; all those who practice it have a good understanding. His praise endures forever!"* And in Proverbs 9:10: *"The fear of the LORD is the beginning of wisdom, and the knowledge of the Holy One is insight."* Notice the word *"understanding."* The fear of the LORD leads to good understanding, while our own understanding, which we've been discussing, is generally opposed to God's will and purposes. Only God can give us proper understanding.

But what does it mean to *"fear the LORD?"* Some years ago when I was writing on the book of Proverbs, I developed an acronym that should hopefully aid in our understanding of what it means to fear God: "F-E-A-R."

"F" for Faith

"Faith" in Christ has been interpreted by some in church history as a mere belief in a set of facts about Christ. But the true faith we're talking about here, and as we stated as we began our study, is resting completely in God's strength, character, and promises. Biblical faith is a synonym of trust. Only one thing will eradicate idols from our lives—complete trust in God's love for us and His ability to perfectly direct our paths, our subject in chapter 4. When I was a new Christian, I liked to think of myself in a deep pit or well. I could only see the light at the top. Everything else was pitch black. I had to call out to God above, who sees everything perfectly, and ask Him to be my guide through the troubles that had surrounded me. He did. Looking back I can see His loving power and guidance, and because of that, my faith—trust—in Him has grown.

God wants nothing more than for us to trust Him—and Him alone—for our lives, both now and for eternity. That is primary. If we trust God completely, all other trusts will be subordinate to that one trust. God is our heavenly Father who sent His Son to die on the Cross for everyone who would simply believe on Him, trusting Him for salvation (John 3:16). He died for you personally, and we can have absolute assurance of our eternal life with Him, which has begun already at our new birth by His Spirit. We aren't saved by our own labors, or good works. What joy! What love! What rest is ours through what Jesus has done for us! Why would we want some other thing in addition to that? Through faith, we are to trust Christ alone for His every good gift (James 1:17), even if the gift He gives isn't the gift we asked for or wanted.

"E" for Enjoyment.

Conservative Presbyterians look to the Westminster Confession of Faith for guidance in theological matters. The Westminster Shorter Catechism's first question is: "What is man's chief end?" In other words, what is the central purpose for which God created us? Westminster's answer is simply: "To glorify God and to enjoy Him forever." Trust in God brings great joy, knowing that He is all-powerful and all-good, and that He loves His children with a perfect love. We can enjoy His great gifts to us, particularly in His gift of His Son, our Lord and Savior, Jesus.

In addition to joy, trust in God brings contentment. Proverbs 19:23 says, *"The fear of the LORD leads to life, and whoever has it rests satisfied; he will not be visited by harm."* Paul says the same thing in Philippians 4:12-13, *"I know how to be brought low, and I know how to abound. In any and every circumstance, I have learned the secret of facing plenty and hunger, abundance and need. I can do all things through him who strengthens me."* Paul's idea is reiterated by today's Baptist pastor and teacher John Piper, who says: "God is most glorified in us, when we are most satisfied in Him." Not only does our enjoyment of God bring glory to Him, but it also means that we know that all things are from His hand for our eternal benefit. We can enjoy God because He is the God who keeps His promises even though sometimes they may seem too good to be true.

My dad, although a wonderful Christian man, worried a lot. He died a young man at 51 years of age. I've always believed that worry and anxiety were partly to blame. Trust in God should eliminate worry and fear from our lives. Paul asks two rhetorical questions in Romans 8:31b-32: *"If God is for us, who can be against us? He who did not spare his own Son but gave him up for us all, how will he not also with him graciously give us all things?"* Enjoying God, in part, is the sure knowledge that no one or no thing can be against me, and that God will graciously give me all things that I need for life, now and forevermore.

"A" for Active Obedience

When we come to Christ in saving faith, we are given a desire to obey His commands. Jesus says repeatedly, *"If you love me you will keep my commandments"* (He says this four times in John 14 alone!) In other words, obedience and love for Christ are axiomatic: you can't have one without the other. You can't love Christ without obedience to Him. *Active* obedience means that we obey joyfully, not because we have to, but because we want to. Unlike a son who obeys his parents after they ask him to take out the trash for the eighth time, an actively obedient son will take the trash out without being asked. His motive? He wants to please his parents because he loves and respects them.

Many believe that God's law for the Christian is restrictive, but as we'll see later, God's law is given to bring us true freedom. The psalmist says in Psalm 119:35, *"Lead me in the path of your commandments, for I delight in it."* I love God's law, and also see it as pure delight. Over the years, I've studied the Proverbs and written about them. In the Proverbs, God shows us how to walk in this path of true freedom, avoiding life's traps and the many sorrows unbelief and idolatry can bring. Living by God's law brings enjoyment, satisfaction, freedom from life's traps, and a life free from the fears of unbelief, a wonderful benefit of being a Christian.

Another of the most wonderful things about being a Christian is that we report solely and directly to King Jesus. Yes, we do respect and obey our church elders and pastors, as they are Christ's under–shepherds (Hebrews 13:7). We are also required to obey the civil authorities (Romans 13:1). But if anyone orders us to do anything that conflicts with the Bible, then we must only follow God's Word, reporting in active obedience to the one and only great King.

Finally, "R" for Reverential Awe

I have never liked horror movies, although they are very popular. I prefer a good comedy or an adventure story. Horror movies play against our human insecurities, fears for our safety, and our propensity to be terrorized. There is a real sense for unbelievers that the true God is terrifying. That's perhaps one reason they don't want anything to do with Him. But as one of God's children, to fear God is quite different. He is our heavenly Father, and promises us that no ultimate harm can come to us. To hold the almighty and eternal God in reverential awe is a great joy.

God resides in awesome majesty. Yes, He's our Friend, and our Father, but if we were face-to-face with Him, we would be down on our faces before Him in recognition of our low estate. Like the prophet in Isaiah 6:5, we would say, *"Woe is me! For I am lost; for I am a man of unclean lips, and I dwell in the midst of a people of unclean lips; for my eyes have seen the King, the LORD of hosts!"* Our God is an awesome God, and we fear Him as a child fears his earthly father—with respect, admiration, honor, and a desire to do his will. The fear of the LORD is the beginning—the first-fruits—of godly wisdom, the wisdom that frees.

So the cure for idolatry—worshiping the creature rather than the Creator—is trusting in the one, true God, as opposed to all other things that seek to turn us away from Him. Let's turn now to a brief discussion of a few idolatrous misconceptions that many Christian hold.

Luck, Chance, and Superstitions

Any discussion of idolatry should briefly address superstition. I believe that idols can be labeled as small or large. In the Bible idols are sometimes referred to as gods—small "g," while the true God is spelled with a capital "G." Similarly, It helps to classify idols into groups, large idols and small idols, and maybe even medium-sized idols. A large idol would be one that totally consumes one's life. If that large idol were threatened, the idolater would experience extreme devastation. I would spell that Idol with a capital "I." We also trust small idols, but they do not so consume a person's life as much as ultimate Idols do. I would spell that idol with a small "i." What we are talking about in superstitions, such as the concept of "luck," are usually idols with a small "i." But regardless of whether an idol is small or large, all idolatry is an offense against our holy God.

Luck and Chance

Many Christians believe in the pagan concept of "luck." We often hear people say, "Good luck!" in circumstances where they wish someone well. "Luck" or "fortune" is supposed to be a force that operates for either good or evil in life. Luck, like "chance," may be understood to be a power of some sort that shapes events or opportunities. If someone says, "You were lucky to get that job!" it makes luck out to be an external energy that may be influenced by what an individual says or does. The problem is that the Bible teaches no such concept. There is no such thing as "luck." God is absolutely sovereign over His creation. Nevertheless, many Christians operate in their daily lives as if "luck" were true. When they do so, they bow down to the idol (small "i") of superstition.

The only ultimate power that exists in the universe is the power that is held by the God of Scripture. All other powers are contingent upon His will and ordination. In the Great Commission of Matthew 28:18b, Jesus says, *"All authority in heaven and on earth has been given to me."* And again, in His answer to Pontius Pilate in

John 19:11a: *"You would have no authority over me at all unless it had been given you from above."* Jesus is claiming that there exists no power or authority or force that isn't contingent upon God's power and control—His providence. Therefore, no such thing as a force or power called "luck" exists. In a former church of ours, just to drive home the point, we held a monthly dinner which we jokingly referred to as a "pot providence," rather than a "pot luck."

Nevertheless many people, including Christians, observe certain rituals that they believe will influence events and opportunities. If we were walking down the street together, my mother would not allow a post or telephone pole to come between us. If one did, she would say, "Bread and butter!" That was to ward off any disagreements that might ensue from the separation supposedly caused by the pole. She wouldn't walk under a ladder, as she considered it to bring bad luck. And, of course, almost everyone knows that to break a mirror brings seven years of bad luck. Just as God saw the needs of the Israelites when they were in bondage in Egypt, He sees our needs and moves to accomplish His will for our lives regardless of our "luck" or "unlucky" actions. If it weren't so, Romans 8:28 would not be true: *"And we know that for those who love God all things work together for good, for those who are called according to his purpose."*

More Superstitions

In America, baseball has been called our national pastime. Baseball players are notorious for their superstitions. If a player goes on a hitting streak, he may not change his underwear for as long as the streak lasts. Some may carry medallions or charms they think will bring luck. A rabbit's foot is well-known for supposed luck. In Asia, numbers are associated with good luck. For instance, the number "8" is thought to bring good fortune. People have been known to pay thousands for a license plate, or home address, that prominently displays the number 8 or some other lucky number. My brother married a woman from Taiwan years ago. The wedding gifts of money were all presented to Bill and his bride in red envelopes. One would never use white! In China, red is the lucky color that brings life. White means death. If you go into a Buddhist temple, the first thing you notice is the burning incense and food left by the worshipers. These gifts are superstitious artifacts that seek to influence luck for the individual worshiper.

Astrology

We all can easily find a column on astrology in our daily newspaper, evidence that many people believe that human activities are somehow controlled by the sun, moon, and stars. Many evangelical believers read the astrological columns daily, and take them into account in their daily activities. Like luck and chance, this is a superstition that the Bible condemns as idolatry (Isaiah 47:13-15, for instance). In Deuteronomy 4:19 we read, *"And beware lest you raise your eyes to heaven, and when you see the sun and the moon and the stars, all the host of heaven, you be drawn away and bow down to them and serve them, things that the LORD your God has allotted to all the peoples under the whole heaven."* Though it is probably a small "i" idol, the Bible clearly teaches against the use of astrology to guide one's life. As we've discussed, to worship an idol is to trust in something or someone other than the living God. It is to base your identity and value on the creature rather than the Creator. Therefore, superstition, the idea of luck or fortune and astrological forecasts, are all forms of idolatry, but not as powerful as the idol to which we now turn: legalism.

Legalism

The most prevalent form of idolatry in Christian circles is legalism. We'll be looking at various types of legalism as we move along, but let me for now give you a very simple definition. Legalism, as it pertains to idolatry, is attempting to do for oneself what God has already done in Christ Jesus. In other words, legalism is attempting to earn one's salvation, or become closer to God, by one's own good works. We've already mentioned this wonderful hymn that's in many Christian hymn books: "Jesus paid it all, all to Him I owe. Sin has left its crimson stain, He washed it white as snow." That's the Gospel. Legalism is attempting to add to Christ's finished work. It is trusting in one's own work and thereby denigrating the finished work of Christ. And it is the most prevalent form of idolatry both now and in antiquity. Legalism is a most insidious and deadly form of idolatry.

One American pastor, Chuck Swindoll, has written, "Legalism is an attitude, a mentality based on pride. It is an obsessive conformity to an artificial standard for the purpose of exalting oneself. . . Legalism says, 'I do this or I don't do that, and therefore I am pleasing God.'" The big problem with legalism is that it distorts the free Gospel of our Lord Jesus, while at the same time it distorts the love and power of our heavenly Father in salvation. Legalism also distorts God's love shone forth in His law. God's law for the Christian isn't something to bring fear. God's law for the Christian is his friend, designed by God to guide us to live productive, fruitful, and joyful lives. To place God's law as a burden upon our shoulders is to distort the God of free grace into a heavenly tyrant who stands ready to pounce upon any Christian who dares not live up to His standards. Of course, God disciplines those He loves (Hebrews 12:6f). But that discipline is always done in love for our own welfare, and to restore us to joyous fellowship.

Another type of legalistic thinking can also require conformance to rules that are extra-biblical. The idea is that some people want to propagate rules that aren't found in the Bible, requiring others to behave according to those rules or supposedly sin against God. Colossians 2:20-22 speaks of these rules: *"If with Christ you died to the elemental spirits of the world, why, as if you were still alive in the world, do you submit to regulations—'Do not handle, Do not taste, Do not touch' (referring to things that all perish as they are used)—according to human precepts and teachings?"* It is perfectly fine for an individual to hold a conviction about some rule that he finds helpful for him or her. For instance, some have found it extremely helpful in their understanding of the Bible and in their walk with God, to read through the Bible every year. But that is their own conviction. They might encourage you to do it, but if they command you to do it and say, "Well, you're not much of a Christian if you don't read through the Bible once a year. You won't be blessed by God," they are practicing this form of legalism. It could be a rule about dress, about eating or drinking, a rule about the Sabbath day. . . anything that's not specifically taught in Holy Scripture. You can see how such a rule can become an idol that enslaves oneself and others. The legalist believes that his own good works can either provide the basis of his or her salvation or closeness to God. This is idolatry because those who practice legalism are trusting in their own actions instead of trusting fully in God's loving-kindness and grace in salvation.

Presuppositions and Traditions

Another form of idolatry that falls under legalism is to place some idea or presupposition above Scripture. We must view the world and every "fact" through the lens of God's holy Word. But often we find folks looking at Scripture through worldly things, causing them to make Scripture say what they want it to say. The Pharisees and Sadducees placed their tradition above God's Word and interpreted Scripture according to their man–made traditions. Jesus said of the Jewish leaders in Mark 7:13: *"[You are] thus making void the word of God by your tradition that you have handed down. And many such things you do."* Roman Catholics do the same by viewing church tradition and the Magisterium's decrees as equivalent or superior to the Bible. Mormons have added to Scripture their *Book of Mormon* and *Pearl of Great Price*, books that are used to reinterpret and therefore nullify God's Word.

We evangelicals can do the same by way of our preconceptions and presuppositions. The Bible then takes a back seat to these man–made documents, traditions, or presuppositions. Rather than God's Word interpreting these books, traditions, and presuppositions, it has become the other way around. One such presupposition has arisen recently in what is called, "Open Theology." It is the false notion that the Bible teaches that God can and does change His mind. The notion arises from verses like Jonah 3:10 where the Ninevites repented: *"When God saw what they did, how they turned from their evil way, God relented of the disaster that he had said he would do to them, and he did not do it."* By this verse and a few more like it, the proponents of Open Theology do violence to the overwhelming number of verses in the Bible that teach that God knows the future exhaustively and doesn't change His mind. For instance, *"And also the Glory of Israel will not lie or have regret, for he is not a man, that he should have regret"* (1 Samuel 15:29). As we'll see in the next chapter, God is omniscient. The future lies before Him like an open book. God ordains whatsoever come to pass. God had to know all along that the Ninevites would repent. We must be very careful to let Scripture interpret Scripture. We all need to beware of this phenomenon of building a doctrine out of one isolated verse or passage.

We also may be moved to make an idol out of so-called "science" like evolution. The theory of evolution isn't science, it's history. No one but God knows the truth. He was there when creation happened! And He has given the truth of origins in the Bible. But many today interpret the Bible according to their idol of evolutionary theory and try to accommodate a man-made presupposition to God's Word.

Finally, in our look at *"our own understanding,"* we should address the way many of us live our daily lives. While we acknowledge God and look forward to being with Him for eternity, we live like pagans. As we've said earlier many of us are "red light" atheists—functional atheists. Even though we say we trust God for all of our needs, we function as if He doesn't exist. Instead, we should have a day-to-day understanding that God directs every aspect and every moment of our lives. To live the life that God has for us, we should let God be in control and allow Him to take us wherever He wants us to go. He is our eternal heavenly Father, knowing us much better than we know ourselves.

The secret is to give up control and let God have the steering wheel. I'm not saying that we should become "quietists," and not give our shoulders to the effort. But we must let God's Spirit and His Word be our firm Resource, Guide, and Power. We will never regret it. God loves His children with a perfect love and He has our best interests at heart, even when the going gets tough and He seems distant from us. In doing so, we will not be leaning on our own sinful understanding, and our lives will be gloriously blessed.

Believers are called to seek God and His glory and to acknowledge Him in all our ways, the subject of our third chapter. In other words, we are to know God and trust Him completely because of that knowledge, asking Him to allow all our needs, wants, and desires to be fulfilled in Him alone. That is the only way idols may be contained and ultimately destroyed in the Christian life. God calls His people to become "idol destroyers." We are to ingest the truth of the One true God, through His Word and Spirit, and become His warriors in the great battle to save souls from idolatry and ultimate destruction. That's our business. That said, let us now turn to the next phrase of our two verses, *"in all your ways acknowledge Him."*

Questions for Further Study

1. Read Genesis 6:5-8. We spoke of Noah and the Flood earlier. In verse 5, what does the Lord say about the hearts of men and women in Noah's time? Why do you think Noah wasn't among them? What does verse 8 say about Noah that made him different?

What made the difference?

2. Read Genesis 8:21. What does God say about the human heart? Why is it that everyone carries this same evil heart? Wouldn't you think that some folks would be good?

3. Read 1 Samuel 15:23. Saul sinned against Yahweh by not doing what God told him to do. My Bible says he was arrogant. Why do you suppose "arrogance" or "stubbornness" is compared to "idolatry"? What had Saul rejected? What does God require of kings and us? If we don't, is God right in calling us "arrogant" or "stubborn?"

4. Read Psalm 14:1-3. We see here man's same common sinfulness in these verses. What is the central core issue? (Hint: It's in the first part of verse 1.) What do you think the "good" would be in verse 2b? What will God do about mankind's problem in vs. 7?

5. Read Ezekiel 36:25-26. Who is speaking? What is the speaker promising to do? What is the change he will cause to happen in the human heart?

6. Read Jonah 2:8. The NIV says, "*Those who cling to worthless idols turn away from God's love for them.*" The KJV says, "*They that observe lying vanities forsake their own mercy.*" Think of these two different translations. How are idols like "lying vanities?" How is God's love like His "mercy" or "grace?"

7. Read Romans 1:18-32. Who is "they" (v. 21a) of whom Paul is speaking? What is their sin? What are the results? In what ways today do we worship created things?

8. Read Romans 3:10-23. To whom do these verses apply? Is anyone good, short of God's intervention? Continue reading Romans 3:21-26. What has God done to correct the problem? On what basis does He do this? (See verse 26b).

9. Read 1 Corinthians 10:14-22. In verse 14, Paul tells us to flee from something. What is it? Later in verse 21 he tells us ***why*** we are to flee. What is Paul's reason?

10. Read Revelation 21:8. Who is speaking? What is the fate of all idolaters? What other sins does He compare to idolatry?

Chapter III

"In All Your Ways Acknowledge Him"

THE HEART DETERMINES A MAN'S WAYS. But suppose a person's heart is divided between the things of God and the things of the world? That is what James called "*...a double-minded man, unstable in all he does*" (James 1:8b). He's got one foot in the world, guided by the flesh and the world system, and one foot in God's Word, guided by the Holy Spirit. He twists this way and that. The "*double-minded*" man lacks a focused direction. In the 1950's, Ella Fitzgerald sang a popular song called *Undecided*. The lyrics went like this, "First you say you do, and then you don't, and then you say you will, and then you won't, you're undecided now, so what are you gonna do?" That's the double-minded man. He can't make up his mind which way to go, and when he does decide, he probably has made the wrong choice.

One of the first things we notice as we begin Proverbs 3:6 is the symmetry between the "*all your heart*" of verse five, and "*all your ways*," here. The harmony is, of course, designed. It is an example of the aspect of Hebrew poetry called "synthetic parallelism," where the second phrase of a proverb supplements or completes the thought of the first phrase. The heart is the core of man's being—the very center of his will and decision-making. One's ways are guided by what the heart dictates. If one's heart is fixed on the Lord and guided by His Spirit, one's ways will naturally follow Him in grateful, joyful, active obedience. Alternatively, if one's heart is fixed on things of the world system—the fallen flesh—his walk will be characterized by those lusts and passions, and his obedience will be grudging and forced. Attempting to explain what caused him to engage in a incestuous tryst some years ago, the comedian and filmmaker Woody Allen accurately stated, "The heart wants what it wants."

We walk through life in many "ways," following many callings. For instance, I have been a son, a student, an army officer, a salesman, a husband, a father, an employee, a business owner, a church elder, a teacher, an author, and a grandfather. And that's just to name the highlights (or lowlights) of my "ways."

While we all wear many "hats" as we walk though this life, Solomon is emphasizing that our trust in God affects all of life—all of the many hats that we wear. We don't merely live as Christians on Sunday in our worship activities, and then live like the world the other six days. We trust God not only to lead us in worship—that we may worship Him in spirit and in truth—but in our moment-by-moment walk each and every day. We are to take God's Word and its wisdom, and live that wisdom out minute by minute, trusting God in everything we think, say, and do, giving Him all the glory.

So now we encounter the command to *"acknowledge Him in all your ways."* What does it mean to acknowledge God? I remember when I was in high school we would walk (or run) from one class to another. During those times the halls were crowded and we would see many friends or classmates coming in the opposite direction. Usually, we could only say a quick, "Hi!" to acknowledge their presence and their friendship. But woe to you if you missed someone! People would begin to think you didn't like them or that you were "stuck up" or too conceited to acknowledge them. But you were in a hurry! Your mind was on that chemistry exam! But this isn't what Solomon means by saying we must "acknowledge" God. We don't just casually tip our hats to Him in a crowded hallway. It's much more than that.

Proverbs 3:6a is basically saying this: "In every way that makes up your life, acknowledge God for who He has revealed Himself to be." Earlier, we looked at the fact that our *"own understanding"*, the understanding that arises from our sin nature, will lead us into worshiping false gods—trusting created things rather than the Creator. We also talked about the "false god" of legalism, saying that legalism was perhaps the most insidious form of idolatry. But there may be one form of idolatry that exceeds even legalism in its heresy. The worst form of idolatry is to make a false god out of the one true God. In our *"own understanding"* we often do exactly that. We either ignore or even deliberately twist the character or essential attributes of the Creator of the universe. Of course, we can't know God perfectly. But we are to receive and believe what can and should be known about Him through His holy Word, through the life of Jesus Christ, and through that which He has created. To do otherwise is to fashion a false god out of the one true God.

The Smörgåsbord Approach

Amy and I used to occasionally eat at a resort hotel nearby our home that served a wonderful smörgåsbord of delightful foods. The tab to go through the buffet line was quite high, and I'm one of those people who thinks I have to eat a lot of the best stuff because I've paid so much. So, I look for the most expensive and tasty dishes: raw oysters on the half shell, gulf shrimp, roast beef, and desserts of every imaginable flavor. I usually bypass the stuffed bell peppers and the Brussels sprouts.

Often, we may be tempted to think of God's character and attributes in the same way—like a smörgåsbord or cafeteria. We will take some goodness and grace but pass on His justice and wrath. We like His omnipotence—His great power—but may turn up our noses at His sovereignty—His willful, precise rule over His creation. We pass over characteristics like God's omniscience and His omnipresence, preferring instead God's loving-kindness and eternity. What Solomon is saying in Proverbs 3:6a is that to know God, we must believe in and trust in **all** of His attributes and divine character. And, of course as John says in 1 John 2:3: *"And by this we know that we have come to know him, if we keep his commandments."* We acknowledge God primarily in our obedience to His revealed will, and recognition that He is so much more than what we would imagine if left to our own preferences.

God's Two Ways of Self-Revelation

God has revealed Himself to mankind in two important ways. First, God reveals Himself in what He has created. Second, He reveals Himself in His Words—both His written Word, the Bible—and the living Word, our Lord Jesus Christ. Regarding creation, Paul tells us in Romans 1:20; *"For [God's] invisible attributes, namely, his eternal power and divine nature, have been clearly perceived, ever since the creation of the world, in the things that have been made. So they are without excuse."* Paul is saying that men and women everywhere, since the creation to the present day, can know that the true God exists just by looking at the world around them. This is called God's *general revelation*. What kinds of things can anyone know about God from what He has made? First, we can know that God must be eternal. The most basic question in all of philosophy is this: "Why is there something rather than nothing?" The most foundational rule of science is the law of cause and effect. For every effect—and the universe and you and I are effects—there must be a first Cause. For something to exist today, something—some One—must have the power of existence within Himself and not require a cause for His existence. In other words, the Creator has to be an eternal Being. He must have existence before anything else can have existence. God is the first Cause, and all of creation is the effect of God's cause. Jesus alludes to this eternal existence in John 5:26 when He says: *"For as the Father has life in himself, so he has granted the Son also to have life in himself."* In other words, Jesus is claiming to have the quality of aseity—eternal existence.

The next thing the creation tells us about the Creator is that He has enormous power. Think of nature—the sun, the stars, the earth, the powerful oceans, and the incredible variety of living things. Think of your eyes which see in color and are set apart to provide us with depth perception. Think about your hands and their opposable thumbs which allow you to do a multiplicity of tasks well. Your skin—and your entire body for that matter—has a marvelous ability to constantly renew itself. Think of your other senses, your nose and ears and sense of touch.

Your imagination is a wonderful gift that mimics God's imagination as evident in His creation. Think of your ability to reason and dream of the future. I have artistic friends with wonderful creativity. Where did it come from? The answer is that you and I have "person-hood"—we're persons with personalities. Where did that come from? Our personalities come from a God who has personal Being. Since we, His creatures, are persons, God must have person-hood Himself.

In creation, we also see God's beauty. He's a good God filled with divinely perfect artistic ability. He's a God of infinite understanding of physics, chemistry, mathematics, biology, astronomy—fields of inquiry in which we mortals have merely scratched the surface. There is so much to know about God from what He has made. But look around us and we see warfare, terrorism, murder, divorce, racism, all kinds of evil. Why? Is God an evil creator? There are those Gnostics who would have us believe that. But to understand why the world is the way it is we must go to God's second form of revelation—His Word, or His special revelation, the Bible.

God's Self-Revelation in the Bible

The first chapters of Genesis are at the center of the Christian's understanding of the rest of the Bible. In other words, the rest of Scripture is but a footnote that gives an explanation of the first three chapters of Genesis, and how God is resolving the great tragedy of Genesis 3. In those first three chapters, we have the narrative of creation and mankind's subsequent fall. God created a very good universe, and populated it with very good things. So, why isn't everything good now? We also have the answer for that in Genesis. The first man and woman sinned against their Creator and plunged the world into spiritual darkness and physical decay and death. A curse came upon the entire universe because of Adam's sin. But then, in Genesis 3:15, we have these words of God speaking to the Serpent—Satan: *"I will put enmity between you and the woman, and between your offspring and her offspring; he shall bruise your head, and you shall bruise his heel."* This verse is sometimes called the *proto–evangel*. It is the first instance of the Gospel message: The woman's offspring will restore the world to its pristine goodness and destroy the *"god of this world"* (2 Corinthians 4:4) in the process. It is about the coming One who will die for the sins of His people—our Lord Jesus Christ. So in these three short chapters we have the entire scope of Scripture in seed form: Creation, Fall, Redemption, and Restoration.

Must we wonder at why the world seeks to deconstruct the first chapters of Genesis? Men, in their natural state, apart from the spiritual resurrection that the new birth graciously brings, want nothing to do with a holy God. So, they invent ways to get rid of Him. We are told things like, "The universe wasn't created by some supernatural power. It is the result of billions of years of evolutionary progress powered by chance. That's a scientific fact!" If you think about that statement for two minutes—maybe even one minute—you'll see its astonishing irrationality. First of all, and as we've said before, evolutionary theory isn't a scientific theory, it's a theory of history.

Scientists may cause fruit flies to mutate in a lab experiment, but the fruit flies are still fruit flies. There is not one whit of scientific evidence that a species can "progress" into another species. When fossils are found in the earth, they are always identifiable as a particular species and not what has become known as "the missing link." There is no missing link. No missing link will ever be found. So, if you want to know something about the history of the universe, why not ask someone who was there when it began? We have His report in the first three chapters of Genesis. Space doesn't allow us to have a full discussion of creation versus evolution, but I have provided a number of good texts in the bibliography at the end of the book. Suffice it to say that any theory that would take glory from the Creator and His infallible Word should be anathema to the Christian, to say nothing of honest, rational, common sense.

Will we believe God or won't we? To "acknowledge" God is to believe who He is and what He has said and to follow Him in loving obedience. It is to believe His Word. Many scientists today—unlike Isaac Newton and scientists of past eras—begin their investigations using a materialistic presupposition. That is, they begin by eliminating any possibility of the supernatural—any possibility of a Creator God. "Creationism is religion, not science," they say. In modern man's humanistic philosophy, man, not God, is the measure of everything. If one begins an investigation of facts with an erroneous presupposition that eliminates or distorts possibilities, his conclusions will also be distorted or completely erroneous.

We must learn to think as the Apostle warned his protégé, Timothy: *"O Timothy, guard the deposit entrusted to you. Avoid the irreverent babble and* **contradictions of what is falsely called "knowledge,"** *for by professing it some have swerved from the faith..."* (1 Timothy 6:20-21). Paul is speaking of those who distort the truth of God's Word by some esoteric, yet false, *"knowledge."* That's the kind of thing being espoused by today's evolutionary scientists. My hope is built on God's sure Word and not on false presuppositions that destroy all hope. I hope that's true for you too.

The God Whom We Are To Worship

Let's look closely now at the God whom we worship. I'll attempt to present a short, but biblically accurate picture of who He is. We'll do this by looking at both God's general and special revelation—both created things and God's living Word. We'll divide our study into two parts: God's moral character—those attributes of God which human beings may share—and His incommunicable attributes, those which God alone possesses. These are attributes that aren't shared with any creature. Volumes of books have been written regarding the person and work of God. I won't attempt to do more than to present a brief sketch, but I have provided a detailed bibliography in the appendices that will guide further study.

I have also attempted to show in the discussion of each topic how our Lord Jesus exhibited God's attributes in His earthly ministry. Of course, Jesus not only exhibited God's perfect moral character, but His great power and knowledge as well. God's mighty power and great love, displayed primarily on Calvary's cross, brought *"many sons to glory"* (Hebrews 2:10).

Acknowledging God's Moral Character

Two further thoughts before we begin: First, I have not given you a complete list of God's attributes, but only those I believed to be most important to our study. God has many more qualities, both moral and personal. Second, as you read and ingest God's moral qualities, compare your own thoughts and actions with those of God—Father, Son, and Holy Spirit. I know I fail miserably. But instead of driving myself to despair, I remember that this God to whom I can't come within a million miles of comparing myself morally or in any other sense, loves me and gave Himself for me. But we are not without hope for moral perfection, for when He takes us home, *"we shall be like him, because we shall see him as he is"* (1 John 3:2d).

God is Holy

> *"...but as he who called you is holy, you also be holy in all your conduct, since it is written, "You shall be holy, for I am holy" (1 Peter 1:15-16).*

One way we "acknowledge" God is by knowing and understanding His character. I would define "character" briefly as the sum of a person's moral qualities. Our God is a holy God—set apart from His creation in both His being and His righteousness. In other words, God is holy both in His supernatural, ontological, metaphysical nature, and in His righteous character. In Isaiah we find these words:

> *"In the year that King Uzziah died I saw the Lord sitting upon a throne, high and lifted up; and the train of his robe filled the temple. Above him stood the seraphim. Each had six wings: with two he covered his face, and with two he covered his feet, and with two he flew. And one called to another and said: 'Holy, holy, holy is the LORD of hosts; the whole earth is full of his glory!'"*
> (Isaiah 6:1-3).

One of the ways that the ancient Hebrew writers emphasized a point was to use repetition. You may recall Jesus preceded several of His statements by the words, "*Verily, verily.*" (KJV), or "*truly, truly.*" (ESV) (Unfortunately, in some of today's modern translations, those original Greek words, "Amen, amen" are often translated "*I tell you the truth...*" John 5:24 for instance in the NIV.) Jesus was using repetition to emphasize the great truth of what He was about to say. It's as if He was to say, "Listen up! What I have to say is really important!" To say something twice was to heighten its truth or its importance. But to say it three times, as the seraphs said "*holy, holy, holy*" in Isaiah 6:3, is to compound the emphasis and raise it to ultimate status. Our God is a holy, holy, holy God—ultimately holy.

The *Evangelical Dictionary of Theology* defines God's holiness in this way:

> "God is distinct from and transcendent to all his creatures, not only metaphysically (His ultimate nature) and epistemologically (His knowledge), but also morally. God is morally spotless in character and action, upright, pure, and untainted with evil desires, motives, thoughts, words, or acts. God is holy, and as such is the source and standard of what is right."

Human beings were created to bear this spotless image of God. We read in Genesis 1:26-27,

> "*Then God said, 'Let us make man in our image, after our likeness. And let them have dominion over the fish of the sea and over the birds of the heavens and over the livestock and over all the earth and over every creeping thing that creeps on the earth.' So God made man in his own image, in the image of God he created him; male and female he created them.*"

In theological terms, God's image in man is called in Latin the *imago dei*. As we discussed earlier, when we fell in Adam's sin, part of God's image in man became disfigured. This is sometimes called the structural, material, or the broad image of God in man. It involves things like our ability to speak, to reason, and our personal, physical resources that allow us to operate in the world. These things were severely damaged. For instance, we came under the curse of death. The other part of the *imago dei*, sometimes called the functional or narrow image, included mankind's moral ability. This part of God's image in man was completely destroyed. We came under the bondage of sin and became God's enemies. We became selfish and destitute of any ability to do good: that is, to acknowledge and glorify God in all of our ways.

Christ came to restore the *imago dei* in God's people and to remove the curse that God had pronounced upon sin. To do this, He lived a perfectly "*holy, holy, holy*" life and then died for our sins and was resurrected for our ultimate justification through faith in Him. Therefore, while Christians can never share in the metaphysical holiness of God, we are called to be of His holy character. Recalling 1 Peter 1:15-16, *"...but as he who called you is holy, you also be holy in all your conduct, since it is written, 'You shall be holy, for I am holy.'"* The functional image of God will not be completely restored in us in this life. But we have His promise that it will be when we see Him in person, face to face in heaven.

Jesus exhibited God's holy character every second of every day that He walked upon the earth as a man. Not tainted by original sin through the miracle of the Virgin Birth, and driven on by His Father's love, Jesus obeyed His Father's will perfectly. This fact is so important, yet ignored by godless critics in books, plays, and movies like *The DaVinci Code*, which depict Jesus as a mere man like the rest of us, with His own lusts and sinful passions. These critics seek to destroy the biblical truth that only a "*holy, holy, holy*" God could take human sin upon Himself in full payment for its debt and guilt. The writer to the Hebrews states so clearly in Hebrews 10:10 & 14: *"And by that will we have been sanctified through the offering of the body of Jesus Christ once for all. . . For by a single offering he has perfected for all time those who are being sanctified."* The first way we are to acknowledge" God is to revere Him as perfectly holy and righteous. We are to acknowledge His ultimate holiness.

God is Good

"The LORD is good, a stronghold in the day of trouble; he knows those who take refuge in him" (Nahum 1:7).

David says in Psalms 25:8, *"Good and upright is the LORD; therefore he instructs sinners in the way."* And again in Psalms 34:8: *"Oh, taste and see that the LORD is good! Blessed is the man who takes refuge in him!"* Have you ever noticed that when the "good times roll," and things are going well, God is never mentioned. But if a hurricane inundates New Orleans with seawater or a tornado devastates some small town in Alabama, it's an "act of God." And that's right—hurricanes *are* an act of God. But He never brings a hurricane or an earthquake or a tornado or any other natural disaster to bear upon His creation for evil purposes. Everything God does is good. This truth is difficult for a believer to understand and entirely impossible for the unbeliever to understand. But it is absolutely true. God detests evil, yet He is long-suffering and compassionate toward His creation. God acts only in accordance with who He is. God cannot do anything contrary to His nature of holiness and righteousness. He always does what is right. God is good.

In Luke 18:18-19, a certain ruler asked Jesus, "*'Good Teacher, what must I do to inherit eternal life?'* And Jesus said to him, *'Why do you call me good? No one is good except God alone.'*" Jesus's answer must have shocked the man, as it also must shock us. Jesus was not saying He wasn't God. He was asking the ruler, "Do you think I am God?" When we compare ourselves to our fellow humans, perhaps I could say, "Well, I'm a pretty good man." But compared to God, my "goodness" is like a rotten toothpick compared to a 500 year old redwood! If I was really a good man, I would love God with all my heart mind soul and strength every second of every day of my entire life. As it is, although I want to do that, I can't keep it up for five minutes. If we were really good, we would glorify God every second of our lives, both before and after our salvation.

Jesus perfectly exemplified genuine goodness in His earthly walk. He had compassion on the sick and crippled and healed their infirmities. He fed the poor and prayed constantly for God's kingdom, and did not succumb to Satan's temptations. He walked every moment with His good Father. It was impossible for Jesus to do anything but good, as goodness is the core of His nature as God. Many in the Church today see Jesus only as a good example for us. Though it is true that Jesus is our perfect example, in a larger sense these folks disparage Christ's ultimate goodness. He lived in goodness, died and rose again, so that many might know the real goodness of God. And through the power of His Spirit, Jesus is transforming into good people those who have put their trust in Him. Apart from Christ, however, we are *"only evil continually"* (Genesis 6:5d).

God is Just

"Thus says the LORD: 'Let not the wise man boast in his wisdom, let not the mighty man boast in his might, let not the rich man boast in his riches, but let him who boasts boast in this, that he understands and knows me, that I am the LORD who practices steadfast love, justice, and righteousness in the earth. For in these things I delight, declares the LORD'" (Jeremiah 9:23-24).

When we think of justice, we normally think of a criminal being sentenced to a proper punishment for the crime he committed. We might say, "justice has been served." Certainly God is very interested in that form of justice. But in Jeremiah and other prophetic books of the Old Testament, God reveals Himself to be a God of justice in another, very important sense. For instance, we read God's words in Isaiah 10:1-2, *"Woe to those who decree iniquitous decrees, and the writers who keep writing oppression, to turn aside the needy from justice and to rob the poor of my people of their right, that widows may be their spoil, and that they may make the fatherless their prey!"* God is very concerned about the treatment of orphans and widows and of the alien, the poor, and the oppressed. Many of us in America have had such incredible material blessings. And yet many are poor and homeless. We hide behind generalizations that they must be feckless, or lazy, or drunkards. But that is only a smokescreen that reveals our true nature: for the most part, we are not really concerned with God's justice.

Our Father is a God of absolute justice. He can't merely slam down His heavenly gavel and declare men and women innocent without someone paying the penalty and absolving the guilt of their sin. Someone asks, "Well, why can't God just forgive and forget? Why does He demand satisfaction for our sins against Him?" Think about it for a second. Suppose someone steals money from you. Let's say that you confront the thief and he asks for your forgiveness. You want and need your money back, but the thief can't pay, he's already spent it. So you decide to forgive the man and forget the incident. He doesn't pay, but you do! You take the loss. It's the same way with our heavenly Father. We owe too much to ever repay our debt of sin. So God took the loss Himself. He sent His Son, Jesus Christ, to pay the price.

John says in 1 John 1:9: *"If we confess our sins, he is faithful and just to forgive us our sins and to cleanse us from all unrighteousness."* Sin is any infraction of God's law, of His righteous character. On what basis does God forgive us? On the basis that His Son, the pre–existent Creator of the universe, became a man and died for the sins of His people. Jesus submitted Himself to a sinner's death so that you and I and everyone who trusts in Him alone for salvation, might **not** be the recipients of God's justice. He took the hit for us, and much more! Instead of hell, we receive heaven. Instead of an eternity of disintegration and hopeless despair, we receive an eternity of endless joy. Sin can only be healed by God's grace, and His grace always brings us to saving faith in Jesus's life, death and resurrection. The cross is the preeminent evidence of God's justice.

Jesus perfectly exhibited His Father's justice in other ways as He walked the dusty roads of Israel and Galilee. He fed the poor and treated them with kindness and mercy. Jesus spoke about the poor often. One time at a banquet, He noticed how the guests were finely dressed and seated at the tables in places of honor. He said to the host, *"But when you give a feast, invite the poor, the crippled, the lame, the blind, and you will be blessed."* (Luke 14:13-14a). In another place, Jesus told of a Samaritan's kindness and said, *"Go and do likewise."* When we are kind to the poor and oppressed, we acknowledge God's justice.

God is Impartial

"So Peter opened his mouth and said: 'Truly I understand that God shows no partiality, but in every nation anyone who fears him and does what is right is acceptable to him'" (Acts 10:34-35).

I've often heard the statement in business that "It's not **what** you know, it's **who** you know." In other words, to get somewhere in life, it's most helpful to know men or women of power who can move you forward. Unfortunately, that's often true in this world of ours. But not with God. He shows partiality to no one. As Paul says in Romans 2:6-11:

"[God] will render to each one according to his works: to those who by patience in well-doing seek for glory and honor and immortality, he will give

eternal life; but for those who are self-seeking and do not obey the truth, but obey unrighteousness, there will be wrath and fury. There will be tribulation and distress for every human being who does evil, the Jew first and also the Greek, but glory and honor and peace for everyone who does good, the Jew first and also the Greek. For God shows no partiality."

When God chose Israel to go into the Promised Land, it was not because of some foreseen righteousness or goodness they possessed. It was because of His covenant with Abraham and the Patriarchs. Hear these words from Deuteronomy 9:5-6 as Yahweh speaks directly to the nation:

*"Not because of your righteousness or the uprightness of your heart are you going in to possess their land, but because of the wickedness of these nations the LORD your God is driving them out from before you, and that he may confirm the word that the LORD swore to your fathers, to Abraham, to Isaac, and to Jacob. Know, therefore, that the LORD your God is not giving you this good land to possess because of your righteousness, **for you are a stubborn people**."*

God is accomplishing His purposes in this world with people whom He describes in 1 Corinthians 1:26-29:

"For consider your calling, brothers: not many of you were wise according to worldly standards, not many were powerful, not many were of noble birth. But God chose what is foolish in the world to shame the wise; God chose what is weak in the world to shame the strong; God chose what is low and despised in the world, even things that are not, to bring to nothing things that are, so that no human being might boast in the presence of God."

Completely unlike any idol or system of mankind, God doesn't call us or reward us according to our abilities, our gifts, or our standing in the community. He is completely fair and impartial. He offers His salvation as a free gift to all without distinction. Even in God's saving grace, He remains impartial. Salvation is not based on any previous good that God sees in us. Our salvation is based on no previous conditions whatsoever, except that we are great sinners.

Jesus is our model of impartiality. In fact, if He seemed to be partial to any class of people, (and He was not), it was to the poor and the outcast, the tax collector, the prostitute, and sinner. Christ's way of thinking is diametrically opposed to the world's thinking. I'm often convicted that in my sin I am not anything like our Lord.

God is Jealous

> *"Take care, lest you forget the covenant of the LORD your God, which he made with you, and make a carved image, the form of anything that the LORD your God has forbidden you. For the LORD your God is a consuming fire, **a jealous God**"* (Deuteronomy 4:23-24).

The movie and television star Oprah Winfrey has said on more than one occasion that she discarded any belief in the Christian God because she read He was a *"jealous God."* Obviously, she was thinking in terms of a jealous boyfriend or girlfriend who might stalk the object of their affection, trying to see if he or she was cheating. But Oprah didn't understand that God's jealousy is quite different. God's jealousy for His people is for their protection. Like a mother hen cuddling her chicks into her bosom, God seeks the welfare of His little ones. In Exodus 34:14 Yahweh says, *"...for you shall worship no other god, for the LORD, whose name is Jealous, is a jealous God..."* As we have seen in the preceding chapter, idolatry, or worshiping something or someone other than the living God, is perilous for us. Idolatry leads to death—eternal separation from God's love. God wants us to live and not die. God's desire is to free His people from slavery to sin. He is a jealous God and His jealousy accrues to our benefit. We should give thanks for God's jealousy! Even when the going really gets tough, even if our very lives are threatened, God's jealousy guards us in unfailing love.

Jesus exhibited God's jealous character in dealing with the Pharisees and teachers of the law. He reviled them in no uncertain terms, calling them a *"brood of vipers"* and bringing down dreadful woes upon their heads (See Matthew 23). Why? What were they doing that so enraged our Lord? They were perverting His Gospel. Israel's leaders were misrepresenting the purpose of God's law and leading God's people into a path of false legalistic righteousness. They were *"blind guides"* who thought they were being faithful to God, but in reality they were opposing God's will and way. We see the same kind of false prophets in our day. Jesus said in Matthew 7:15, *"Beware of false prophets, who come to you in sheep's clothing but inwardly are ravenous wolves."* One brand of false prophet promises things like health, wealth, and total fulfillment of your dreams in this world. How do we spot them? Know your Bible. Understand that God hasn't ever promised us a rose garden in the here and now. On the contrary, Jesus said in John 16:33b, *"In the world you will have tribulation. But take heart; I have overcome the world."* C.S. Lewis said, "If you think of this world as a place intended simply for your happiness, you find it quite intolerable: think of it as a place of training and correction and it's not so bad." Don't be fooled by false prophets.

God is Wrathful

"And that night the angel of the LORD went out and struck down 185,000 in the camp of the Assyrians. And when people arose early in the morning, behold, these were all dead bodies" (2 Kings 19:35).

God's wrath is part of His moral attributes. God's wrath is His righteous, holy, and just response to sin. But we must never equate God's wrath with human anger and wrath. God's wrath is always just. Man's wrath is rarely just. Befitting God's perfectly just and loving character, sin must be judged and punished. Sinners are not only under the guilt of sin, but under its load of insurmountable debt as well. When Jesus went to the Cross, He paid the believers' unrepayable debt of sin as well as He took upon Himself our cosmic, infinite guilt of sin. He suffered and died for all who would ultimately trust Him for salvation. Those who remain outside His gracious and effective accomplishment must suffer as He did, not for the sins of others, but for their own sin. Jesus paid the entire price for our salvation. Those outside His loving bond will sadly never be able to finish paying for theirs.

Paul tells us in Romans 2:5-6, *"But because of your hard and impenitent heart you are storing up wrath for yourself on the day of wrath when God's righteous judgment will be revealed. He will render to each one according to his works."* The word Paul uses for "wrath" is the Greek word *orgys*. It is the word from which we derive the word "orgy." God's wrath is real and it is furious. Hell isn't necessarily the absence of God. It is the absence of His mercy and loving–kindness. Many preachers today hesitate to talk about the reality of God's wrath, wanting to be politically correct, I suppose. In the final analysis, as C.S. Lewis so correctly said, "There are two kinds of people in the world. Those who say to God, 'Thy will be done.' And those to whom God says, 'Thy will be done'" (*The Great Divorce*).

It should be noted that while God shares all of His moral characteristics, communicable attributes, with mankind, He has commanded us specifically to leave wrath to Him and Him alone. For as we read in Hebrews 10:30-31, quoting Deuteronomy 32:25-36: "For we know him who said, *"Vengeance is mine; I will repay."* And again, *"The Lord will judge his people. It is a fearful thing to fall into the hands of the living God."* We are to leave revenge in God's hands. He will repay everyone according to their deeds (Romans 12:19). That doesn't mean that the police and courts have nothing to do. God has given government the "sword" to punish evildoers in this evil world.

Jesus displayed God's wrath in overturning the tables of the money changers and animal sellers in God's Temple (Mark 11:12ff). God's holy place was being transformed into a den of robbers, and Jesus's reaction was swift and harsh. Fearing Him, the chief priests and teachers of the law sought to kill our Lord.

God is Wise

> "Daniel answered and said: 'Blessed be the name of God forever and ever, to whom belong wisdom and might. He changes times and seasons; he removes kings and sets up kings; he gives wisdom to the wise and knowledge to those who have understanding; he reveals deep and hidden things; he knows what is in the darkness, and the light dwells with him'" (Daniel 2:20-22).

Even though we may share in God's wisdom, His wisdom far surpasses any wisdom of the world. We read these words from the Apostle Paul in 1 Corinthians 1:22-25:

> "For Jews demand signs and Greeks seek wisdom, but we preach Christ crucified, a stumbling block to Jews and folly to Gentiles, but to those who are called, both Jews and Greeks, Christ the power of God and the wisdom of God. For the foolish-

ness of God is wiser than men, and the weakness of God is stronger than men..."

God's wisdom has been revealed in the Lord Jesus Christ and in His holy Word—our Bible. It has also been revealed in creation. The depth and width and height of the wisdom of God is infinite. How to we recognize wisdom? Wisdom is basically the application of truth to what a person does. Wisdom is proved by right or wrong by what wisdom does. As Jesus said in Matthew 11:19: *"The Son of Man came eating and drinking, and they say, 'Look at him! A glutton and a drunkard, a friend of tax collectors and sinners!' Yet wisdom is justified by her deeds.'"*

Everything God does reflects His infinite wisdom. Men and women scoff at the Cross. Satan was completely taken off guard by the spectacle of God's Son crucified. No doubt he thought He had won a great victory. Little did he realize that the Cross sealed his doom. God knows the beginning from the end. As we shall see later, His knowledge extends throughout time. God knows the future because He ordains whatsoever comes to pass. Because He knows the future exhaustively, only God can discern true wisdom from foolishness. What earthly wisdom could possibly compete?

Jesus exemplified godly wisdom in everything He said and did. Many today and throughout history look on Jesus as a foolish man. Recall the mocking words of those who crucified Him. *"So also the chief priests, with the scribes and elders, mocked him, saying, 'He saved others; he cannot save himself. He is the King of Israel; let him come down now from the cross, and we will believe in him'"* (Matthew 27:42). What they couldn't comprehend was that Jesus was enduring the wrath of His Father for the salvation of untold millions. This was the ultimate moment of all human history, and yet the "wisdom" of sinful men arrogantly mocked the true wisdom of God. Short of God's saving work, we still do it today. Seek God's wisdom. It is available to anyone who will simply ask for it (James 1:5).

God is Love

"Whoever confesses that Jesus is the Son of God, God abides in him, and he in God. So we have come to know and to believe the love that God has for us. God

is love, and whoever abides in love abides in God, and God abides in him"
(1 John 4:15-16).

Love in the biblical sense is unselfishly wanting what is best for others. Jesus speaks of the love of God in John 3:16, *"For God so loved the world, that he gave his only Son, that whoever believes in him should not perish but have eternal life."* Paul also testifies to the love of God in Titus 3:4-5: *"But when the goodness and loving kindness of God our Savior appeared, he saved us, not because of works done by us in righteousness, but according to his own mercy, by the washing of regeneration and renewal of the Holy Spirit."* That great chapter on love in 1 Corinthians gives us the best biblical definition of God's love: *"Love is patient and kind; love does not envy or boast; it is not arrogant or rude. It does not insist on its own way; it is not irritable or resentful; it does not rejoice at wrongdoing, but rejoices with the truth. Love bears all things, believes all things, hopes all things, endures all things. Love never ends"* (1 Corinthians 13:4-8a). Because of His love for us, our God will never fail us. That is huge reason why we can trust Him with all of our heart.

Jesus is the central witness of biblical—*agape*—love, in all of human history. Paul reminds us in Ephesians 5:1, *"Therefore be imitators of God, as beloved children. And walk in love, as Christ loved us and gave himself up for us, a fragrant offering and sacrifice to God."* And as Jesus says in John 15:13, *"Greater love has no one than this, that someone lay down his life for his friends."* The "friends" of which Jesus speaks were His former enemies. This is God's love: so powerful as to turn bitter enemies into loving friends. Do you doubt, Christian friend, that Jesus loves you? Merely look on His cross and see how great His love is for those on whom He has set His affection.

God is Gracious

"For by grace you have been saved through faith. And this is not your own doing; it is the gift of God, not a result of works, so that no one may boast. For we are his workmanship, created in Christ Jesus for good works, which God prepared beforehand, that we should walk in them" (Ephesians 2:8-10).

God's grace is a foreign concept to this wicked world. One of the most clear and full statements of God's grace toward men is in Ephesians 1:1-7, the verses immediately preceding the above:

"And you were dead in the trespasses and sins in which you once walked, following the course of this world, following the prince of the power of the air, the spirit that is now at work in the sons of disobedience—among whom we all once lived in the passions of our flesh, carrying out the desires of the body and the mind, and were by nature children of wrath, like the rest of mankind. But God, being rich in mercy, because of the great love with which he loved us, even when we were dead in our trespasses, made us alive together with Christ—by grace you have been saved—and raised us up with him and seated us with him in the heavenly places in Christ Jesus, so that in the coming ages he might show the immeasurable riches of his grace in kindness toward us in Christ Jesus."

Look at the grace of God like this: A man comes into your home while you are away and steals your valuable coin collection. Not only that, but he murders your family and sets fire to your house, completely destroying it. He is caught and jailed. You go to him and voluntarily take his place in the cell, setting him free to go. Then, you give him your 401k, your IRA, and all the money in your bank account. That is metaphorically speaking what Christ has done for us. God's grace isn't just "unmerited favor." Grace is not getting what we deserve, yes, but what's more, grace is getting exactly the opposite of what we do deserve!

I have a favorite story about a young man who was standing before the elders of his church, giving them his testimony as to why he should be admitted to the Lord's Table. He said to them, "My salvation was a joint effort between God and me." The elders' ears perked up and they asked the young man, "How is this so?" The youth answered, "Well, you see, I did the running away while God did the saving!" That's also what grace is. We run away from God until God draws us to Himself by His grace. This is what Paul means in Romans 5:6-8:

*"For while we were still **weak**, at the right time Christ died for the **ungodly**. For one will scarcely die for a righteous person—though perhaps for a good person one would dare even to die—but God shows his love for us in that while we were still **sinners**, Christ died for us."*

By God's magnificent grace, we who are powerless, ungodly sinners are turned around to run not from Him, but toward Him! We find mercy and love instead of justice and wrath. Instead of eternal death, we find life everlasting.

I realize that many Christians think that if God only saves some and not all, He is being unfair—unjust. But we forget that God is not obligated to save anyone. Left to ourselves, all people are God's cosmic enemies, and blinded to His Gospel by Satan's power, (2 Corinthians 4:4). It is impossible for anyone to be saved without God first opening their spiritual eyes in regeneration and then giving them saving faith (Ephesians 2:8-9). So if God doesn't do the saving, no one would be saved. God would remain perfectly just. God's gracious call extends to all people everywhere, but His effectual call goes out to only those who are being saved, for no other reason but that God loves us and sent His Son to die for us. The Romans 5:6 word "powerless" in the NIV, or "without strength" in the KJV, or "weak" here in the ESV means that we had no capability of repenting before God, by His Spirit, resurrected us to new life in Christ.

I know that this may be a difficult teaching, and we don't have room to deal with it as we should. But if you can see it, that God's sovereign grace logically precedes your faith in Christ, the entire Bible will come alive as never before. After 19 years of struggle with the issues of God's sovereignty in election, I came to the full realization that I have been saved only by God's work in my heart and not by anything that I did for myself, not even a decision I made over 40 years ago.

A form of God's unmerited kindness also extends to those who hate him and never will want anything to do with Him. In the Reformed tradition a distinction is made between God's "saving grace" and what has been called His "common grace." I prefer the term "common kindness" or "common mercy." Either way, the word "common" doesn't mean the way we usually understand that term, as mediocre or inferior. Common kindness means that it is a kindness that is shared with all humanity. Jesus gives us an example of common kindness in Matthew 5:43-45: *"You have heard that it was said, 'You shall love your neighbor and hate your enemy.' But I say to you, Love your enemies and pray for those who persecute you, so that you may be sons of your Father who is in heaven. For he makes his sun rise on the evil and on the good, and sends rain on the just and on the unjust."* God is kind to those who are perishing, but it is not a saving kindness. It is common to all men everywhere who at present aren't getting what they really deserve. Instead, they are getting air to breathe and food to eat and families to love. In eternity, such kindness for the unbeliever will vanish.

Jesus is the ultimate picture of God's grace in action. He came into a world of enemies, most of whom had no reason to expect grace. Then, in perfect righteousness, Christ died for His enemies. He calls each of His followers now to do the same. We are to live for our enemies. We are to respond to Jesus's command of Matthew 28:19-20 and, *"...go and make disciples of all nations, baptizing them in the name of the Father and of the Son and of the Holy Spirit, and teaching them to obey everything I have commanded you. And surely I am with you always, to the very end of the age."*

God is Merciful

"He has told you, O man, what is good; and what does the LORD require of you but to do justice, and to love kindness, and to walk humbly with your God?" (Micah 6:8).

As one might expect from a good, loving God, His goodness and love overflow into mercy for His creatures. Quoting David again, we read these words in Psalms 25:6: *"Remember your mercy, O LORD, and your steadfast love, for they have been from of old."* And as Jesus commands us in Luke 6:36: *"Be merciful, even as your Father is merciful."* That said, God's ultimate mercy extends only to those who put their trust in Him, for as Mary says in her Magnificat, *"His mercy extends to those who fear him, from generation to generation"* (Luke 1:50). My favorite word in the Bible is the Hebrew word *hesed*. It is often translated "loving-kindness." Our God is a merciful God full of *hesed*—loving-kindness. Our God is a forgiving God, ready to forgive our sins as we confess and repent of them. But His mercy and forgiveness isn't free. It cost Him dearly.

We spoke of God's grace earlier, the grace by which we are saved. What's the difference between God's mercy and His grace? They are very closely related in my mind. If there is a real difference, it is perhaps this: Mercy is the province of God and men that heals earthly wounds and relieves our suffering. Mercy spares us the punishment we deserve. Grace is God's attribute that heals sin and its effects. Grace provides us with the opposite of what we've earned. We participate in the distribution of God's mercy through the alleviation of hunger, disease, and earthly human needs. We participate in the distribution of God's grace through the effectual heavenward call of God's Spirit through the ministry of the Gospel.

That our Lord Jesus was merciful in His earthly ministry goes without saying. His mercy to broken men and women began with His incarnation and continued right up to the time He was taken into heaven (Acts 1:9). As our Lord told John the Baptist's disciples in Luke 7:22: "*Go and tell John what you have seen and heard: the blind receive their sight, the lame walk, lepers are cleansed, and the deaf hear, the dead are raised up, the poor have good news preached to them.*" A woman was caught in adultery. Jesus rejected the accusations of those who brought charges and told her "*go and sin no more*" (John 8:11b). The examples of Christ's mercy to others are almost beyond counting. His mercy continues today, of course, as He reigns in power from His heavenly throne, answering our prayers and healing our infirmities and suffering.

God is Patient

"Do you suppose, O man—you who judge those who practice such things and yet do them yourself—that you will escape the judgment of God? Or do you presume on the riches of his kindness and forbearance and patience, not knowing that God's kindness is meant to lead you to repentance?" (Romans 2:3-4).

In 2 Peter 3:9 the disciple and apostle speaks of Christ's second coming and the end of the age: "*The Lord is not slow to fulfill his promise as some count slowness, but is patient toward you, not wishing that any should perish, but that all should reach repentance.*" We know by experience that many do not come to repentance, even though God's patient, merciful hands are outstretched to them. Therefore the term *"everyone"* here, must not mean everyone without exception, but without distinction. There will come a day soon when God's call will cease. The calling out of Christ's Church will be complete. The gavel will fall and Christ will come *"to judge the living and the dead"* (1 Peter 4:5).

God is also patient with His people. We are saved, but we are still sinners. Augustine said that we are *simul just et peccator*—"at the same time justified yet sinners." We must make every effort to be obedient and faithful, not to accomplish our own salvation, but to please our heavenly Father and not presume upon His patient nature. When I was a brand new Christian years ago, I was advised never to pray for patience because God would bring difficulty into my life to teach me the virtue by my suffering. I was already in trouble up to my ears and didn't need any more. But God did teach me patience through it all. Oh, I still have my bouts with impatience, but I've learned to trust Him, even when the traffic lights turn red!

What patience Jesus exhibited with those around Him as He ministered on this earth. Have you ever thought of how our Lord must have suffered every day he was on the earth. He was sinless, yet He walked for 33 years in the midst of rank sinners, knowing every moment of every day the death that awaited Him. One would think He would have become vexed or exasperated at every turn. But no. Our Lord dealt gently and patiently even with those who sought to murder Him.

Conclusion

What is God's goal for every Christian? We have already answered the question elsewhere, but Paul says it best in Romans 8:29: *"For those whom he foreknew he also **predestined to be conformed to the image of his Son**, in order that he might be the firstborn among many brothers."* God's goal for His children is for each of us to be conformed to the image of His Son—our Lord Jesus. How are we to understand what that means outside of what God has said in His Word? The goal of sanctification, which the Holy Spirit is producing in our lives even now, is to change us into Christ's image. Someday, we know that we will be like Him in His character, as we will stand glorified in His presence. As John says in 1 John 3:2: *"Beloved, we are God's children now, and what we will be has not yet appeared; but we know that when he appears we shall be like him, because we shall see him as he is."*

In becoming more like God's Son, we are to reflect His righteousness, and reject our own self-centeredness. We are to reflect the moral component of who God is. Forgetting ourselves, we are to live for others in this world of woe. How are we to do that? Are we to tighten our belts, screw up our courage, and march out into the world to follow Christ? That will never work. The only way that we can even hope to bear the marks of Christ-likeness is to rely completely upon His Holy Spirit to guide and direct our lives, and to give us the power to live in accordance with His holiness and righteousness—His perfect law. In our own flesh, we can do **nothing**! The late seminary professor Dr. John Gerstner used to define "nothing" as that which the sleeping rocks dream of. Zero! Our own strength will get us nowhere. Only through being sanctified by the Lord Jesus—filled, strengthened, and matured by His Spirit—can we hope to become more and more like Him (John 15:5).

Acknowledging God's Incommunicable Attributes

While we have just looked at God's attributes of which we may share to some degree with Him, we are also to *"acknowledge"* God for His attributes that are His and His alone. Those are attributes which He cannot share in any way with His creatures. We don't have space to list all of God's incommunicable attributes, nor to pay them the close attention that they deserve. But we must acknowledge our heavenly Father in each of His attributes. Failure to do so will form in our minds a false god—not the God of Scripture. Can we know Him perfectly? No. Can the finite comprehend the infinite? Of course not. But we can know a lot, and God has given us sufficient information about Himself to help us do exactly that. As we study, we'll look at Jesus and try to see how he illustrated these attributes in His earthly ministry.

God is Incomprehensible

"Can you find out the deep things of God?
Can you find out the limit of the Almighty?
It is higher than heaven—what can you do?
Deeper than Sheol—what can you know?
Its measure is longer than the earth
and broader than the sea" (Job 11:7-9).

A theological movement developed in the early part of the 20th Century that said God is "wholly other." In other words, that God is so transcendently above His creatures that any meaningful knowledge of Him is beyond our ability to gather. They said that God can only be described in negative terms—what He is not. It began as a defense of orthodoxy, but fell to resemble liberalism. To Emil Brunner, Karl Barth, and others in the Neo-orthodox movement, God was impersonal and unknowable—much like the gods of Gnosticism and the eastern religions of Hinduism and Buddhism. Well, we might concede an element of truth in their view, in that God is transcendent, and not a part of His creation. However, by God's appointment, we **can** know things about God—lots of things—not only from His Word, but also from what He has made (Romans 1:20-21).

When we say that God is incomprehensible, we mean that God is beyond our knowing Him comprehensively—completely. The finite cannot fully comprehend the infinite. Even in eternity, we will not be able to fully grasp God's complete being, wisdom, and knowledge. As Paul says in his benediction of the discussion of God's perfect will in Romans 11:33-34: *"Oh, the depth of the riches and wisdom and knowledge of God! How unsearchable are his judgments and how inscrutable his ways!"* Then he adds the rhetorical questions, *"For who has known the mind of the Lord, or who has been his counselor?"* The answer is, of course, no one. But we can know some things! Lots of things! We can penetrate His character and His attributes as He instructs us in His creation and in His Word.

God has further revealed Himself by sending us His Son—our Lord Jesus. Jesus made the incomprehensible God much more comprehensible as He walked and talked with people just like us. For instance, we would have never understood as well as we do the riches of God's love and compassion had He not sent us the perfect God-Man to display such love and compassion during His ministry and particularly on Calvary's cross. In the New Testament, we have Christ's words and the words of His apostles as they were guided by Christ's Spirit. The mysterious Old Testament comes alive as we are shown how it is all about Jesus. Like the New, the Old Testament is focused on Christ's suffering and glorification—His death and resurrection. We can understand God much more clearly because of Jesus, but we still cannot comprehend God's motivations and things like why He allowed evil to enter the world.

When we say, "God is incomprehensible," there's always the danger of someone saying, "Well, since God is incomprehensible, why should I ever try to understand all of His attributes?" One way I would answer the question is this: "Because to understand the true God, even in a limited way, is the greatest of joys." In America today, there is very little contemplation of God's attributes. We watch a lot of TV and read lots of books, but we don't sit quietly and contemplate our loving God. We're cheating ourselves. To really know the loving, all-powerful God who created and sustains all that exists is to find the greatest of all joys. It is to trust Him more fully, to love Him more dearly, to follow Him more closely, and become more like Christ every day.

God is Infinite

"Do I not fill heaven and earth? declares the LORD" (Jeremiah 23:24).

Amy and I live near a city where the street lights and other reflected lights limit our ability to see the stars at night. But we've been in the middle of Death Valley in California where the stars shine in incredible brilliance and glory. I've tried to fathom the unlimited space of God's creation and fall far short. But space is ultimately limited, and God is not. He is infinite—boundless, endless, completely unlimited. In all of His attributes, God is without limit or restriction. His being is infinite. His wisdom is infinite. His knowledge is infinite. His love is infinite. His sovereignty is infinite. In all of God's attributes, He is infinitely endowed. To limit God in any way is to worship a false god.

As Zophar the Naamathite correctly argued in Job 11:7-8: *"Can you find out the deep things of God? Can you find out the limit of the Almighty? It is higher than heaven—what can you do? Deeper than Sheol—what can you know?"* And as Solomon said in 1 Kings 8:27: *"But will God indeed dwell on the earth? Behold, heaven and the highest heaven cannot contain you; how much less this house that I have built!"* Finally, as the Psalmist states in Psalms 147:4-5: *"[God] determines the number of the stars; he gives to all of them their names. Great is our Lord, and abundant in power; his understanding is beyond measure."* God is limited only by His own character, as we'll see next.

Christians believe that the infinite God took on finite flesh. How is this possible? We don't know—it is a sacred mystery. But Christians must believe exactly that, because only an infinite God could suffer infinitely for His people in the space of three hours time upon the Cross at Calvary. Only an infinite God could have the power to rise from the grave. In many American churches, Jesus is seen only as a godly example for us to follow. What infinite arrogance! What disrespect to view our Savior in such a completely limited way. Well, I cannot comprehend infinity. I look up at the stars in the night sky and try to understand the distance that light travels in a year. A thousand years. It boggles the mind! And yet, though space may model God's infinity, it doesn't approach God's measureless existence. We have an infinite God.

God is Spirit and Truth

> *"But the hour is coming, and is now here, when the true worshipers will worship the Father in spirit and truth, for the Father is seeking such people to worship him. God is spirit, and those who worship him must worship in spirit and truth"* (John 4:23-24).

Amy and I used to live in Asheville, North Carolina. It's a town that is known for its "spirituality." Back in the early part of this new millennium, many Christians displayed bumper stickers that read, "We Still Pray." To counter the obvious reference to God, many unbelievers began to display the bumper sticker, "We Still Chant." Spirituality in Asheville is all about New Agers, witches, warlocks and earth worshiping. Many may think they worship in spirit, but they neither worship in God's Spirit nor in truth. They worship gods—idols—of their own making. Meanwhile, Jesus told the Samaritan woman at the well: *"God is spirit, and those who worship him must worship in spirit and truth."* (John 4:24). Many in Asheville worship gods they do not know. But we worship the one, true God who has made Himself known in His creation, in His Word and in His Son, Jesus Christ. Jesus prays for us in John 17:17: *"Sanctify [your Church] in the truth; your word is truth."*

In today's modern culture, truth has been superseded by so-called "tolerance." Tolerance used to be a civil or political term, meaning that Christians and others were to be broad-minded, lenient, forgiving, and patient with those of different religions and secular views. But today, society has redefined "tolerance." It now supposedly means that all religious and philosophical views are equal in their truth commitments. In other words, it is considered intolerant to claim that Jesus is the only way to eternal life, even if you believe in the freedom of others to disagree with you. Truth is marginalized and even made obsolete in the cause of not offending anyone. Even obvious contradictions are accepted as unimportant in the maintenance of today's tolerance. The whole idea is insanity. Everyone believes in truth. Even the people that say there is no truth believe that their statement against truth is absolutely true. Schools and colleges couldn't exist if the teacher or professor had to be tolerant of error. Of course truth exists, and its origin and essence is found in the God–man, Jesus.

In Jesus Christ, Truth walked the surface of this earth for over 30 years. Over and over again, Jesus prefaced His remarks by phrases like, *"For truly, I say to you..."* (Matthew 5:18, for instance.) Jesus bore constant witness to God's truthfulness. Our Lord not only spoke the truth, He is the truth. He claimed to be God in many words and deeds, and by accepting worship. Jesus would have violated the first commandment if His claim to be God incarnate wasn't true. On one occasion, He said of Himself, *"I am the way and the truth and the life"* (John 14:6). His many miraculous works attested to the truth of His words. How can anyone then listen to Jesus and not believe Him? It's because of human insanity, also known as "sin." People, left in their natural state, don't have the spiritual *"ears to hear"* (Mark 4:23, for instance).

In courts of law, witnesses are sworn to "tell the truth, the whole truth, and nothing but the truth." That's because we humans are prone to lie, particularly when there's a lot at stake. Our courts have stiff penalties for perjury. Thinking God is like us, prone to lie, we humans try to put God in the dock all the time, accusing Him of perjury or doing evil things. What we sometimes fail to understand about God is that He is incapable of doing anything that is contrary to His character. God is altogether good. He speaks only the truth and yet His freedom is unbounded. We'll continue this discussion next.

God is Free

*"I am God, and there is none like me, declaring the end from the beginning and from ancient times things not yet done, saying, **'My counsel shall stand, and I will accomplish all my purpose,'** calling a bird of prey from the east, the man of my counsel from a far country. **I have spoken, and I will bring it to pass; I have purposed, and I will do it.** "Listen to me, you stubborn of heart, you who are far from righteousness: I bring near my righteousness; it is not far off, and my salvation will not delay..."* (Isaiah 46:9b-13).

We in America live in "the land of the free and the home of the brave." In its brief history, the United States has provided its citizens with much freedom of movement and conscience. And yet, we are not truly "free." We are of the earth and bound by our many limitations. I would love to just spread my arms and take off over the hills and valleys near my home, flying without wings. Unfortunately, there's this thing called gravity that prohibits my "freedom" to do that. Societal laws want to prevent my doing 75 in a 35 miles–per–hour zone. Likewise, I am restricted by my economic circumstances, by my age, by my gifts and capabilities, by my genes, my background and upbringing, and by my commitments to God and to others. But like His infinity, God's freedom is not restricted. Let me qualify that. God's freedom is restricted in one important way as we briefly discussed in the last section: He cannot do anything that is in opposition to His holy moral character. He is perfect in His integrity. God cannot do evil. God cannot sin against Himself or His creation, because He is infinitely good. As we've seen, He is *"holy, holy, holy"* (Isaiah 6:3, Revelation 4:8). In St. Augustine's terms, God is *non posse peccare*. That's Latin for "not possible to sin." And yet God is ultimately free to do whatever He chooses to do, but everything He chooses to do is good. So theologians say that God is free to do all that is within His holy will. But God cannot sin.

In the Garden of Eden, Adam was, as Augustine put it, *posse peccare, posse non peccare*. It was possible for Adam and Eve to go either way—to sin or not to sin. While being created *"very good"* (Genesis 1:31), Adam was given free will to choose either the good or the evil. Adam had what's called "the power of contrary choice." (Even the completely free God has never had the power of "contrary choice," as He can only choose good, never evil.) We know that Adam chose to do evil, thinking it would make him free to be like God. What really happened was that Adam and Eve and their descendants ever since have been *non posse non peccare*—not possible **not** to sin. Humans became enemies of God and unable to do anything good (Again, see Romans 3:10-18). Before we are saved we are free to one extent: we are free to make choices, but left to ourselves short of God's regenerating power, we always sin. Sin is bondage for those created in God's image, it's not freedom at all. One consequence of our bondage to sin is our inability to recognize true spiritual freedom.

When the Holy Spirit resurrects our hearts and minds in the new birth, we are changed. Our stony hearts are transformed to hearts of flesh (Ezekiel 36:26). We transition from *non posse non peccare* to *posse peccare, posse non peccare*—able either to sin or not to sin. We're back where we were in the Garden, except that we retain the sin nature that Adam didn't have when he was created. (But believers also have a very important addition—the Holy Spirit living within us.) When we Christians die and go to be with the Lord, we will be changed into persons who will live eternally with the *non posse peccare* God. We, too, will never be able to sin again, to the praise of His wonderful name.

In Jesus, we see the altogether righteous *non posse peccare* God. He was born free from the sin nature that inhabits all others. He came to the earth that we might have this same freedom. As John says in 8:36 of his gospel, *"So if the Son sets you free, you will be free indeed."* In Galatians 2:4, Paul speaks of *"the freedom we have in Christ Jesus."* Freedom from what? Freedom from slavery to legalism, from slavery to sin, and from the false gods of idolatry. Knowing that God loves us perfectly, we should be free from worry, inordinate fear of the future, etc. In Christ, we come to know the truth, and that truth sets us free indeed (John 8:32). We become free to be the people that God intended us to be originally—truly alive in the image of His Son (Romans 8:29).

God is Triune

> *"Now when all the people were baptized, and when Jesus also had been baptized and was praying, the heavens were opened, and the* **Holy Spirit** *descended on him in bodily form, like a dove; and* **a voice came from heaven,** **"You are my beloved Son;** *with you I am well pleased"* (Luke 3:21-22).

The Bible tells us that the one true God exists in three Persons. The core belief of the Old Testament Jew is called the *Shema*, meaning "hear," and refers to verse 6:4 in Deuteronomy. *"Hear, O Israel: The LORD our God, the LORD is one."* And then verse 5: *"Love the LORD your God with all your heart and with all your soul and with all your might."* Early Christians (and even we today) were accused of worshiping three gods—as polytheists—not just the one true God. The Hebrew Scriptures—our Old Testament—give evidence to the triune nature of God, but it is scant. In Genesis 1:26, the speaker is definitely plural. *"Then God said, 'Let us make mankind in our image, in our likeness.'"* (See also Genesis 1:26). Some have interpreted these verses as a "majestic plural" since kings often speak in the third person plural—"we." But then in Isaiah 42:1 we read these words: *"Behold my servant, whom I uphold, my chosen, in whom my soul delights; I have put my Spirit upon him; he will bring forth justice to the nations."* The speaker is God the Father. He refers to the coming Messiah, promised since Genesis 3:15. The third person mentioned is the Spirit of God. So we have in Isaiah 42:1 Father, Son, and Holy Spirit. This verse is recited in Matthew 12:18 as being a fulfilled prophecy of Isaiah in Christ Jesus. The New Testament is full of references to the holy Trinity.

For instance, we read in 1 Peter 1:1-2:

> *"Peter, an apostle of Jesus Christ, To those who are elect exiles of the Dispersion in Pontus, Galatia, Cappadocia, Asia, and Bithynia, according to the **foreknowledge of God the Father**, in the **sanctification of the Spirit**, for **obedience to Jesus Christ** and for sprinkling with his blood: May grace and peace be multiplied to you.."*

Why is the Trinity important? The notion that God exists in three Persons has also been criticized as being illogical. But it does not defy the law of non-contradiction. If the Bible taught that there are three gods in one god, that is a logical contradiction. But three persons in one God is not a contradiction. God has revealed this truth to us in His Word, and while it is a great mystery, we nevertheless believe it because God has revealed it to us very clearly.

On the other hand, a unitary god, such as Allah of the Muslims, has a fundamental problem. In order to show forth love, he needs to create an object of his love. Allah would therefore become subject to the creature in order to demonstrate his love. If God was required to do or need anything, He would not be truly free. But the true, trinitarian God needs nothing outside of Himself in order to show His love. The three members of the Trinity exist in perfect harmony and mutual love. Our God is a relational God and He has designed those created in His image to be relational beings. To precisely describe the Trinity is impossible. It remains a mystery to us. All we can do is try something like this: The Father loves the Son who is the perfect representation of His Father (Hebrews 1:3). The Holy Spirit—the third person of the Trinity—is the Spirit emanating from the Father and Son who lovingly applies Christ's redemptive work to us believers, convicting us of sin, teaching and guiding us.

In Jesus, we see God in a human body. He sits today at the Father's right hand both as God and as a man. He's our God–Man in Heaven. He is but one Person, yet with two natures. Again, this is no contradiction. Jesus walked the earth speaking of His Father, always praying to Him and doing His will. He also testified of the Holy Spirit who He promised would come and lead us into all truth.

In John 14:26, for instance, Jesus says, *"But the Helper, the Holy Spirit, whom the Father will send in my name, he will teach you all things and bring to your remembrance all that I have said to you."* Finally, in the Great Commission of Matthew 28:19, Jesus commands us to *"...Go therefore and make disciples of all nations, baptizing them in the name of the Father and of the Son and of the Holy Spirit..."*

God is Invisible

"To the King of the ages, immortal, invisible, the only God, be honor and glory forever and ever. Amen" (1 Timothy 1:17).

We spoke earlier of Positivism, a materialistic philosophy that proposed that unless something is subject to witness by the senses of sight, hearing, taste, touch, or smell, it doesn't exist. Therefore, according to that premise, God doesn't exist. The sense of sight won't tell us about the biblical God, except that which may be seen in His creation. But both creation and the Bible are very clear that God exists, and that He is invisible. At Mt. Sinai, Moses had this conversation with the LORD:

"Moses said, 'Please show me your glory.' And he said, 'I will make all my goodness pass before you and will proclaim before you my name 'The LORD.' And I will be gracious to whom I will be gracious, and will show mercy on whom I will show mercy. But,' he said, 'you cannot see my face, for man shall not see me and live'" (Exodus 33:18-20).

Though we cannot see God, we can see what God has made, and through that general revelation understand many things about Him. He has also spoken to us in His Word, which communicates that eyes cannot behold Him. For instance, in 1 Timothy 6:15-16, Paul says, *"[Christ]who is the blessed and only Sovereign, the King of kings and Lord of lords, who alone has immortality, who dwells in unapproachable light, whom no one has ever seen or can see. To him be honor and eternal dominion. Amen."* And, in Colossians 1:13-15: *"[Jesus Christ] has delivered us from the domain of darkness and transferred us to the kingdom of his beloved Son, in whom we have redemption, the forgiveness of sins. He is the image of the invisible God, the firstborn of all creation."*

Even though the thrice-holy God is invisible, He has made visible signs to us in the history of redemption. He has appeared in theophanies, such as the pillar of cloud by day and the pillar of fire by night in the Exodus. He has appeared to several men and women in the Old Testament as *"the Angel of the LORD."* I've counted 65 times that the Angel of the LORD is mentioned in the Old Testament. This particular "Angel" is deemed by many to be the pre-incarnate Christ. Then, ultimately, the God–man Jesus appeared in real space and time. What was His word to those who questioned who He was? In John 14:9b Jesus says, *"Whoever has seen me has seen the Father."* Christ is the image of the invisible God (Colossians 1:15).

God is All Powerful, Almighty, Omnipotent

One of my favorite quotes from the Old Testament is from the book of Numbers 11:23. Moses has asked the LORD a pressing logistical question. How can He possibly feed 600,000 men (plus women and children) during their wanderings in the desert? *"...the LORD said to Moses, 'Is the LORD's hand shortened? Now you shall see whether my word will come true for you or not.'"* The image of the invisible God with a short arm or hand is, for me at least, very humorous. Does God not have the strength to do anything that pleases Him? Of course He does! Not only did Yahweh feed the Israelites in the desert, their *"...clothing did not wear out on you and [their] foot did not swell these forty years."* (Deuteronomy 8:4). The Psalmist says in Psalms 147:4-5: *"[The LORD] determines the number of the stars; he gives to all of them their names. Great is our Lord, and abundant in power; his understanding is beyond measure."*

God's great power was very visible in Jesus. He accomplished miracle after miracle. Like when the Israelites were fed in the desert, Jesus fed thousands out of a few loaves and fishes (Matthew 14:13-21). He walked on the sea, raised the dead, and turned water into fine, aged wine. Ours is the all–powerful yet loving God of our salvation, who created the universe and who will soon recreate the heavens and the earth—a new home for those who are His called ones (Isaiah 65:17). I cannot close this section without the words of Jesus in Matthew 19:26: *"...with*

God all things are possible." Our God is the Almighty One, the King of creation.

What a wonderful thing it is to be a child of the all-powerful Creator God! Whenever I feel a little down and think things are not going my way, I think of God and His amazing, unlimited power and I'm revived. I am wicked beyond my imagination, and yet loved far more than I could ever hope to be. God reached down and brought me to Himself in His Spirit's miracle of regeneration (John 3:3). I'm not too many years from leaving this old earth and joining Him in heaven—a temporary stopover until the Lord comes again with great power and brings with Him *"a new heaven and a new earth, where righteousness is at home"* (2 Peter 3:13). My body may be disintegrated by then, maybe eaten by fish in the sea, maybe burned up in a fire, but He will resurrect my body to be like His glorious body! (Philippians 3:21). That's the power of our great God!

God is Omniscient, All-Seeing, Understands All Things

"Now the word of the LORD came to [Jeremiah], saying, 'Before I formed you in the womb I knew you, and before you were born I consecrated you; I appointed you a prophet to the nations'" (Jeremiah 1:4-5).

To be omniscient is to have perfect knowledge. God knows all things from beginning to end. All events and supposed secrets are laid open before Him. Nothing surprises our eternal God. God isn't limited by space and time nor in His knowledge of the past or future. Neither is He limited by the sheer volume of information before Him. Consider the words of David in Psalms 139:1-6:

"O LORD, you have searched me and known me! You know when I sit down and when I rise up; you discern my thoughts from afar. You search out my path and my lying down and are acquainted with all my ways. Even before a word is on my tongue, behold, O LORD, you know it altogether. You hem me in, behind and before, and lay your hand upon me. Such knowledge is too wonderful for me; it is high; I cannot attain it."

For the Christian, God's perfect knowledge is a wonderful comfort. God sees our needs before they even arise within us (Matthew 6:32). God knows our struggles and our illnesses (Exodus 3:7). God hears our prayers, even those that remain unspoken. Nothing in us, or in all creation, is hidden from Him. But, the notion of God's omniscience is a terror to the unbeliever. The very idea that the secret things of his sinful heart are all laid out to be judged by a holy God *should* be terrifying to him.

Remember that Jesus was able to read people's hearts. He knew precisely what they were thinking. Matthew speaks of one incident where Jesus is speaking to the teachers of the law: *"But Jesus, knowing their thoughts, said, "Why do you think evil in your hearts?"* (Matthew 9:4). One of the clearest statements of God's perfect knowledge is given to us in Hebrews 4:13: *"And no creature is hidden from his sight, but all are naked and exposed to the eyes of him to whom we must give account."* And, ponder these words of the LORD as given to the prophet Isaiah:

> *"Remember this and stand firm, recall it to mind, you transgressors, remember the former things of old; for I am God, and there is no other. I am God, and there is none like me, declaring the end from the beginning and from ancient times things not yet done, saying, 'My counsel shall stand, and I will accomplish all my purposes..."* (Isaiah 46:8-10).

God is Immutable, Unchangeable

Jesus Christ is the same yesterday and today—and forever! (Hebrews 13:8).

Open theists, whom we discussed earlier, dismiss the biblical view that God is immutable. But Samuel, under the inspiration of God's Spirit says: *"And also the Glory of Israel will not lie or have regret, for he is not a man, that he should have regret"* (1 Samuel 15:29). In the New Testament, we find the words of the older Testament upheld. Paul speaks of God's immutability in Romans 11:29: *"...for the gifts and the calling of God are irrevocable."* The writer to the Hebrews chimes in. He says in Hebrews 13:8, *"Jesus Christ is the same yesterday and today and forever."* We have already seen the wonderful words of Hebrews 6:17 and 18 which speak of a God who has the future committed firmly in His hands:

> *"So when God desired to show more convincingly to the heirs of the promise the unchangeable character of his purpose, he guaranteed it with an oath, so that by two unchangeable things, in which it is impossible for God to lie, we*

who have fled for refuge might have strong encouragement to hold fast to the hope set before us."

This attribute of God is incredibly important to us. If God could change His mind, or was not able to see the future with perfect vision, then we could not rely upon any of the many promises He has permanently given to us. Perhaps we would get to His judgment seat and Christ would say, "Well, yes, I did once say that you would only need simple child-like faith to enter my kingdom, but I changed my mind and you no longer qualify." Of course, that is ridiculous! Over the years since Christ's crucifixion and resurrection, some off-shoots of the Christian faith have altered God's Word and brought about novel understandings of His Gospel of salvation by grace alone, but God hasn't changed, neither has He altered the Gospel. He will never change because if He did, He would cease to be God.

Back in the 16th century, a Spanish monk named Luis de Molina (1535-1600), like the Open Theists, proposed just such a God who could change His mind. His heresy has sometimes been called "Middle Knowledge," which denies that God knows the future perfectly. Instead, Molinism alleges that God knows all contingencies and merely adjusts to changing circumstances. Molina said that God knows all the ways that different events could take place, so He can react to changes brought about by human free will. Many modern Christians have adopted Molina's theory in saying that God has "Plan A, Plan B, Plan C," and so on. Molinism was adopted by the Council of Trent and remains a Roman Catholic doctrine to this day. But the Bible gives the heresy no support.

So, how does God's absolute will intersect with man's free choice? It seems like a contradiction to say that God ordains whatever happens, and yet people are ultimately culpable for their decisions. It is a mystery to the finite human mind, but Scripture tells us it is true, and the two wills work in perfect harmony. If God could change His mind, how could *"...we know that for those who love God all things work together for good, for those who are called according to his purpose"*? (Romans 8:28). The Reformers in the 16th century returned to the biblical doctrine of God's perfect knowledge, and called the supposed difficulty, "The Doctrine of

Concurrence." Their understanding was codified in the Westminster Confession of Faith, which states in Ch. 3:1:

> "God from all eternity, did, by the most wise and holy counsel of His own will, freely, and unchangeably ordain whatsoever comes to pass: yet so, as thereby neither is God the author of sin, nor is violence offered to the will of the creatures; nor is the liberty or contingency of second causes taken away, but rather established."

In Jesus coming to this earth as a man, we see God's eternal plan carried out precisely. God's plan of salvation by faith in Jesus had its beginning before time began. The plan was executed thousands of years later in the fullness of time in a tiny country called Israel. God's eternal purpose was carried out by the decisions of evil men who remain culpable for those decisions. God's purposes and His faithfulness to those purposes will never fail. The Psalmist tells us, *"The counsel of the LORD stands forever, the plans of his heart to all generations."* (Psalm 33:11). This means also that God's plans for you and for me will never change. Paul, speaking in God's Spirit says in Philippians 1:6, says, *"And I am sure of this, that he who began a good work in you will bring it to completion at the day of Jesus Christ."* James echoes Paul's words in James 1:16-17: *"Do not be deceived, my beloved brothers. Every good gift and every perfect gift is from above, coming down from the Father of lights with whom there is no variation or shadow due to change."* Finally, these words are from Hebrews 13:8: *"Jesus Christ is the same yesterday and today and forever."*

God is Omnipresent

> *"'Am I a God at hand, declares the LORD, and not a God far away? Can a man hide himself in secret places so that I cannot see him? declares the LORD. Do I not fill heaven and earth?' declares the LORD"*
> (Jeremiah 23:23-24).

When Solomon dedicated the Lord's Temple in Jerusalem, he gave a wonderful speech to the glory of the God in whose honor the edifice was built. He said in 1 Kings 8:27: *"But will God indeed dwell on the earth? Behold, heaven and the highest heaven cannot contain you; how much less this house that I have built!"* We've quoted David in Psalm 139 above in relation to God's perfect knowledge. David goes on to say in 139:7-10, *"Where shall I go from your Spirit? Or where shall I flee from your presence? If I ascend to heaven, you are there! If I make my bed in Sheol, you are there! If I take the wings of the morning and dwell in the uttermost parts of the sea, even there your hand shall lead me, and your right hand shall hold me."* And the Apostle Paul says this of God's omnipresence to the men of Athens in "Acts 17:24-28:

> *"The God who made the world and everything in it, being Lord of heaven and earth, does not live in temples made by man, nor is he served by human hands, as though he needed anything, since he himself gives to all mankind life and breath and everything. And he made from one man every nation of mankind to live on all the face of the earth, having determined allotted periods and the boundaries of their dwelling place, that they should seek God, and perhaps feel their way toward him and find him.* **Yet he is actually not far from each one of us, for 'In him we live and move and have our being';** *as even some of your own poets have said, "For we are indeed his offspring."'*

In Jesus's Spirit, we find God's presence everywhere at once, not in His earthly ministry, but in His role as exalted King of Kings. Jesus confirms in Matthew 18:20: *"For where two or three are gathered in my name, there am I among them."* The Holy Spirit has taken up His home within you. *"If the Spirit of him who raised Jesus from the dead dwells in you, he who raised Christ Jesus from the dead will also give life to your mortal bodies through his Spirit who dwells in you."* (Romans 8:11). We are comforted and emboldened because of God's presence within us and all around us. And we know that He will be with us always, *"...for he has said, 'I will never leave you nor forsake you"* (Hebrews 13:5).

In our church, Amy and I celebrate the Lord's Supper often with our brothers and sisters. In doing so, we believe that Christ's Spirit is with us in what is a divine mystery. The elements of bread and wine speak of Christ's sacrifice on our behalf and we are strengthened in the sure knowledge that we are not alone. Jesus reminds us in the final days of His earthly ministry, *"And behold, I am with you always, to the end of the age"* (Matthew 28:20b). His name is Immanuel, *"God with us"* (Matthew 1:23).

God is Sovereign

"So Pilate said to him, 'You will not speak to me? Do you not know that I have authority to release you and authority to crucify you?'"Jesus answered him, 'You would have no authority over me at all unless it had been given you from above'" (John 19:10-11a).

God's sovereignty is His willingness to rule His creation in minute detail. While His omniscience and omnipotence and His other attributes give Him the ability to reign, God's sovereignty relates to His absolute control over all events. For instance, Paul speaks of God's sovereignty in Romans 13:1-2 and following:

> *"Let every person be subject to the governing authorities. For there is no authority except from God, and those that exist have been instituted by God. Therefore whoever resists the authorities resists what God has appointed, and those who resist will incur judgment."*

If God establishes kings and parliaments and presidents, what other powers exist that He has not established? None whatsoever.

God is not restricted to time and space as we are. God knows the future because He ordains the future and sees it all clearly in front of Him. The writer to the Hebrews says of our Lord Jesus in Hebrews 1:1-3:

> *"Long ago, at many times and in many ways, God spoke to our fathers by the prophets, but in these last days he has spoken to us by his Son, whom he appointed the heir of all things, through whom also he created the world. He is the radiance of the glory of God and the exact imprint of his nature, and he upholds the universe by the word of his power."*

The right hand seat is that of supreme power. Christ is sustaining this earth in such a way that no person could draw another breath were it not for Christ's sustaining and controlling authority. This should be a wonderful comfort to us! The God who loves us perfectly and will not let one hair fall from our heads without His permission, controls our future. To repeat the wonderful words of Paul in Romans 8:28: *"And we know that for those who love God all things work together for good, for those who are called according to his purpose."* How could this be were it not for God's control over all events?

One of the most specific statements of God's sovereignty and rule over His creation is in Isaiah 46, verses 8 through 13:

> "Remember this and stand firm, recall it to mind, you transgressors, remember the former things of old; for I am God, and there is no other; I am God, and there is none like me, declaring the end from the beginning and from ancient times things not yet done, saying, 'My counsel shall stand, and I will accomplish all my purpose,' calling a bird of prey from the east, the man of my counsel from a far country. **I have spoken, and I will bring it to pass; I have purposed, and I will do it.** "Listen to me, you stubborn of heart, you who are far from righteousness: I bring near my righteousness; it is not far off, and my salvation will not delay; I will put salvation in Zion, for Israel my glory."

God's will and providence rule all events. Nothing happens without His foreknowledge and ordination. Many hate this truth because they, like the first couple, want autonomy—to have their own way and live lives apart from the overruling hand of God. But what a comfort for the Christian! Our heavenly Father has all things under His absolute control, and He loves us with a perfect, unchanging love. Though life may seem out of control and filled with disappointment and hardship, we can nevertheless trust that Our heavenly Father is working all things according to His perfect plan.

One of the mistakes we sinful creatures make is to fall too far on one side of a biblical mystery. The Bible teaches that God is absolutely sovereign and yet, at the same time, man is completely responsible for his actions. While we may acknowledge the truth, some of us may fall too far on the side of God's sovereignty. Man becomes almost like a puppet with God pulling the strings. Other Christians may believe that man's responsibility and free will reign supreme. But the Bible teaches that both are equally true and exist in apparent tension with one another. No conflict exists—the two truths exist in perfect harmony. For instance, when Joseph met with his brothers after Jacob's death, the brothers were afraid that Joseph would punish them for selling him into slavery. But Joseph quieted their fears saying, *"As for you, you meant evil against me, but God meant it for good, to bring it about that many people should be kept alive, as they are today"*

(Genesis 50:20). In the same way, Judas and those who crucified Jesus meant to harm Him, but God intended it for good and the salvation of many people. Yet the men who murdered Jesus are still fully accountable for what they did.

One of the characteristics of a cult is its desire to eliminate mystery—apparent contradictions. As we said when we spoke of God's immutability, the Bible's teaching of God's sovereignty versus man's responsibility seems to be a contradiction. But it is not a contradiction, it is a mystery. We might say that it's a "sacred secret." In our finite understanding, we cannot know the mind and capabilities of the infinite God and how he uses human sin to glorify Himself. But we must believe it and give equal weight to both His sovereignty over us and our personal accountability to Him.

In Jesus's life, death, and resurrection, we see God's reign over His creation worked out in this mystery of sovereignty versus accountability. Addressing a crowd in Jerusalem, Peter said, "*...this Jesus, delivered up according to the definite plan and foreknowledge of God, you crucified and killed by the hands of lawless men*" (Acts 2:23). Here we see that God's sovereignty and man's accountability are taught in one verse. God's law is not negotiable. Unbelievers will stand before Christ in the Great White Throne Judgment (Revelation 20:11-15). It is to be a judgment unto condemnation where God will mete out just punishment for each individual's sin. Believers, on the other hand, will not face condemnation (Romans 8:1), but will stand before Christ's Judgment Seat—a judgment unto reward or loss of reward in heaven and on the new earth. Paul states in 2 Corinthians 5:10, "*For we must all appear before the judgment seat of Christ, so that each one may receive what is due for what he has done in the body, whether good or evil.*" He confirms man's responsibility in Galatians 6:7a, "*Do not be deceived: God is not mocked, for whatever one sows, that will he also reap.*"

God is Self-Existent

For the past century or so, the so-called "science" of evolution has been extensively promulgated in America and the world. Space won't allow us to discuss the issues involved, but we actually don't need much space. Besides many other problems faced by atheistic evolutionists, one is insoluble: How did the universe begin? What caused the "Big Bang?" Because of the non-negotiable law of cause and effect, if something exists today, something or someone must have always existed to cause it all. That Someone—the ultimate Cause—is the triune God. Jesus says in John 5:26, *"For as the Father has life in himself, so he has granted the Son also to have life in himself."* In other words, Jesus is not an "effect" like we are, but is the Cause of all the effects that exist. Only Christ supplies the true answer to the question that dogs the pseudo-science of evolution. Christ is the self-existent Creator of the universe.

God is Simple, Indivisible

We've merely scratched the surface of the knowledge of our God. We've covered some basics, but left much more unsaid. One of the most important of all God's attributes is what is called His "simplicity." God is the fullness of all His attributes. To put it in terms that we can understand, to remove or reject one or more of God's eternal attributes is to worship a God who doesn't exist—to worship an idol of our own making. We either worship God as He is—God of both grace and wrath, of both sovereignty and omnipotence, of both perfect knowledge and immutability—or we're worshiping some other god. God's attribute of simplicity is extremely important for us to grasp. We must neither add nor detract from His ontological completeness nor His righteous moral character.

In Jesus, we see a man who is also God. Take away Christ's humanity and He cannot act on our behalf to save us from sin (Hebrews 2:17). Take away His Godhead, Christ could not fulfill all righteousness and He would be stripped of the enormous power necessary to atone for the sins of His people and to impute His perfect righteousness to us. In the same way, to strip God of one of His attributes of character or being is to reduce Him to an idol—a god of our own making.

Conclusion

And so we acknowledge Christ in all of our ways. And what a joy it is for us! We have a great and mighty Savior. Anything less than the almighty and true God would be of no benefit to us. We see Him in His works of creation and in His voice, speaking to us from His Word. He is the mighty God, ruler of His universe. He spoke, and the universe came into being. He continues to speak to guide and provide for His people through the trials and difficulties, through the joys and sadness of this cursed earth. Soon—very soon—Christ will return and a new era of righteousness will be born. A transformed heavens and a transformed earth will be ours. We will work and reign with Him for eternity, blessed far beyond our current understanding.

Questions for Further Study

1. Read Isaiah 6:1-3. What attribute of God are the seraphims celebrating? What does it mean? Why should it bring God glory? In Leviticus 20:7 (and other places), we are told to emulate this attribute. Why?

2. Read Acts 17:31. On what basis will God judge the world? Who will be the judge? What does righteousness have to do with judging?

3. Read 1John 4:7-12. What communicable attribute is spoken of? How would you define this attribute? Do all people without exception have this attribute? If you answered "no," why not? How in history has God shown us the perfect example of what this attribute is and does?

4. Read Ephesians 2:1-10. Which of God's communicable attributes are spoken of in these verses? How are humans described who have yet to experience these attributes? What is the result of God's implementation of these attributes upon us? What has God prepared for them to do in verse 10? Of which of God's attributes does this speak?

5. Read Isaiah 38:7-8. What miracle is performed by God? What happened to the earth? Which of God's incommunicable attributes were at work? Do you really think God has this attribute? Can He do things like this if He wants? How did Jesus display this attribute while on earth?

6. Read Matthew 6:8. Jesus is speaking of God's attribute of omniscience, of perfect knowledge. How does God's perfect knowledge of you bring comfort? Or, does it make you afraid? How does knowing of God's perfect knowledge keep you from sin?

7. Read Hebrews 1:1-3. These verses speak of God's sovereignty over His creation. What does verse 3 teach us about who Jesus is and what He is doing? What does the writer mean by the phrase "all things" in verse 3? Do you think the writer supposed that God had retired to His easy chair?

8. Read Matthew 28:18-20. Three of God's incommunicable attributes are spoken of by Jesus in the Great Commission. Can you find them?

9. Read John 1:1-4. What incommunicable attribute of the "Word" is given to us here? Who is this "Word?" How did He use this attribute in creation?

10. Read John 1:17-18. Which of God's incommunicable attributes does John speak of here? Who has made God known?

Chapter IV

"And He Will Make Straight Your Paths"

One of many Christians' favorite chapters of Scripture is most certainly Psalm 23—a Psalm of David. Laying awake in troubling times, I have gone to sleep reciting that wonderful Psalm more times than I can count. I've gone through long periods of trouble and difficulty in my life, as perhaps you have also. The 23rd Psalm has comforted me in every way. Have you ever noticed that the third verse of that Psalm is almost the same as the fourth stanza of Proverbs 3:5&6? Following the words, *"he restores my soul,"* we read *"He leads me in paths of righteousness for his name's sake"* (Psalms 23:3). The words for "path" are different in the Hebrew in Psalm 23 and Proverbs 3:6. The word which is used in Psalm 23 is the Hebrew word *magal*, meaning a broad path, one which wagons might use. In Proverbs 6, however, the word is *orach*, indicating a road that one might traverse on a regular basis. As one might assume, *orach* is a perhaps more permanent road or path than *magal*. The point is that when you as a believer trust in the LORD with your whole heart and lean not on your own understanding, acknowledging who He is in all of your ways, the LORD places your feet on permanent, unending paths and directs your actions and the events of your life in His will and way.

As I've already mentioned, back in the 1970s and early '80s I was in a deep financial and emotional pit. Actually, it was more like a well or a mine shaft with no ladder to the top. I visualized myself standing in mud and slimy water at the bottom. I couldn't see any "paths." I couldn't see even my hand in front of my face, except when I looked up I saw light. I knew that God was up there and that He could see everything and that He would lift me out of my depression and the financial hole I was in. My emotions were exactly like those of David's, who wrote in Psalm 40:1-3:

"I waited patiently for the LORD; he inclined to me and heard my cry. He drew me up from the pit of destruction, out of the miry bog, and set my feet upon a rock, making my steps secure. He put a new song in my mouth, a song of praise to our God. Many will see and fear, and put their trust in the LORD."

It took several years, but God ultimately lifted me out of that dark hole and placed my feet on solid, high ground. Even though in the pit I couldn't see the wall in front of me, my heavenly Father placed my feet on His path and showed me the way out. Looking back, I never want to visit that deep chasm again. But if He calls me to it, I know my Father will get me through the experience. Also looking back, I wouldn't trade my visit to the black hole for anything in the world. I learned beyond the shadow of a doubt that our God is faithful and He will deliver us!

The word "path" (or "pathway") or its plural, "paths," occur 49 times in the Psalms and Proverbs. That is almost equal to the entire times the word appears in the rest of the Bible. There are nine different Hebrew words translated "path" in the Old Testament and only two Greek words for the subject in the New Testament. In fact, the word "path" (or similar) occurs only thirteen times in the New Testament. Throughout the Bible, we read of narrow paths and wide paths, straight paths and crooked paths. There are righteous paths and there are paths that lead to traps and ultimately to judgment. Here is where the thoughts of David in Psalm 23 and the thoughts of Solomon in Proverbs 3:5&6 converge. They both speak of paths of righteousness. Though we may leave God's righteous path and sin, God puts the true believer's feet back on paths of righteousness and keeps them there throughout his or her walk in this life and beyond. The NIV also uses the word "straight." "*...and he will make your paths straight.*" The KJV and other versions say, "*....and he shall direct thy paths.*" They all mean the same thing: God will make your paths pathways of righteousness.

Listed below are a number of different paths that the Christian may find herself or himself on during their walk with Christ. You will notice that they are not all fun and games. In fact, some like my deep pit experience are frightening and very difficult. Nevertheless, every Christian's path is designed by our God for our eternal benefit and for His eternal glory. Let's begin with the most important, the path of faith, while understanding that these paths overlap one another in the Christian life:

The Path of Faith

The writer to the Hebrews defines a Christian's faith in 11:1: *"Now faith is the assurance of things hoped for, the conviction of things not seen."* Faith deals with unseen and future things. Down in my pit, I couldn't see anything except when I looked up, but I had faith that God loved me and had the power and the purpose to lift me out. My confidence was a bit shaky, and my assurance could have used a pep talk, but I trusted God to bring me out, and He did. In my natural state, I should have quit and died! But I had the hope of deliverance and my hope in God was not in vain. My faith was strengthened by His merciful faithfulness.

In a mere seven words, Paul encapsulates Proverbs 3:5&6 and the Christian life: *"For we walk by faith, not by sight"* (2 Corinthians 5:7). The world walks by what it sees. The Christian walks by what is unseen. We walk by faith, confident in the one true God. We spoke of man's depravity earlier in the book. From their natural appearance to the eye and ear, the vast majority of people look to us as good neighbors, folks who we would like to get to know. But we must walk by what God sees, not what we see. How do we know what God sees? He has given us His Words—the Bible and His Spirit to guide and direct us. Again, I have provided verses on what the Bible says about man as Appendix A. Work through them and ask God to give you a new perspective, not to gloat over mankind's failings, but to see yourself as one of them: a great sinner who by grace alone has a great Savior. This is the path of faith.

The Path of Humility

All of my business career, which spanned almost 40 years, was spent in commercial real estate. There's a wise saying in real estate. The top three factors in determining a property's value are "location, location, and location." In other words, by far the most important and defining factor in the value of real property is where it is located. It's only reasonable that downtown commercial property is worth far more per square foot than commercial property way out in the suburbs. In the same way, Augustine said that the three defining characteristics of the Christian are humility, humility, and humility (*Confessions*).

Ponder these wonderful words of Paul in Philippians 2:5-8:

> *"Have this mind among yourselves, which is yours in Christ Jesus, who, though he was in the form of God, did not count equality with God a thing to be grasped, but emptied himself, by taking the form of a servant, being born in the likeness of men. And being found in human form, he humbled himself by becoming obedient to the point of death, even death on a cross."*

We owe to God's Son our very lives, both now and in eternity. It was He who emptied Himself of His majestic throne in His Father's presence. He came to earth not lying in a golden, silk-upholstered crib, or swaddled in rich, silk garments. He came as a tiny baby, riding on a donkey, sleeping in a animal feeding trough, and wrapped in dusty old blankets. He came on this premise upon which God bases all work that is done for His glory: *"Whoever exalts himself will be humbled, and whoever humbles himself will be exalted."* (Jesus speaking in Matthew 23:12; Luke 18:14).

Christian humility begins with the understanding that our eternal salvation is based on nothing but the grace and promises of a loving God. Our salvation began with the Father's appointment before the creation of the world (Ephesians 1:3-4), it was effectually carried out on the Cross by the humble Jesus who died for His people—His Church (Acts 20:28). Then, in real space and time,

God's Holy Spirit applied to us the salvation already ordained and won, and we were brought from death into life—from darkness into God's marvelous light—through the new birth (Ephesians 2:1).

As Paul makes so clear in Ephesians 2:8-10: *"For by grace you have been saved through faith. And this is not your own doing; it is the gift of God, not a result of works, so that no one may boast. For we are his workmanship, created in Christ Jesus for good works, which God prepared beforehand, that we should walk in them."* The faith that justifies us is not of ourselves, it is the gift of God through the regenerating work of His Holy Spirit. We are to cling only to Christ and Him crucified as a humble Servant. We are to trust humbly in our God and not lean on our own understanding.

Just think! Romans 5:8 says *"...but God shows his love for us in that while we were still sinners, Christ died for us."* The chapter also speaks of us as Christ's godless enemies. We have no reason whatsoever to boast. Just as Jesus humbled Himself, even though He is the all-holy, all-powerful, all-seeing God of the universe, so we also should walk in His ways, for without Him we are eternally lost.

Ultimately, as believers in Christ we are called to give up our "sovereign" will over our lives and allow God to be in command. The unbeliever who wants to be in control of his life hates this. But for the Christian, giving up command and giving it to our loving and almighty Father in heaven is a most wonderful thing. It is the path of humility.

When I learned this truth so many years ago, I eliminated the word "proud" from my vocabulary. As a Christian, I cannot be proud of anything—I can only be thankful. For I have **nothing** that I have not received from God's hand (1 Corinthians 4:7).

The Path of Suffering

False teachers abound in Christendom today. Many falsely teach that "joy" in this life comes in lots of material possessions and good health. Many follow them. Stated simply, the false path is that God wants you to have complete prosperity and complete health now. He doesn't want you to suffer. If you are poor or sick or you suffer in any other way, there must be something wrong with you and your faith. "Certainly it's no fault of God," they might say. "Just have more faith! You can have it all today, if only you have the faith to get it!" According to those who minister overseas, the number of people fooled by this false gospel has grown exponentially in emerging nations in Africa and parts of Asia. The problem with that way of thinking is easy to see. It goes completely counter to everything written in God's Word! While it is true that God does not want His children to suffer for their own sins, or to suffer needlessly, suffering is part of our walk with Him. Just as Jesus suffered for us, so we, too, suffer for Him. Paths of righteousness are paths of suffering. Listen to these statements of Jesus and His Apostles:

Jesus tells His disciples (and us) in John 16:33, *"I have said these things to you, that in me you may have peace. In the world you will have tribulation. But take heart; I have overcome the world."* In Luke 9:22-23 Jesus said, *"'The Son of Man must suffer many things and be rejected by the elders and chief priests and scribes, and be killed, and on the third day be raised.' And he said to all, 'If anyone would come after me, let him deny himself and take up his cross daily and follow me.'"* Have you ever thought of the fact that Jesus' suffering was not restricted to his death, but merely maximized in His crucifixion? He suffered every day of His earthly life. If ever a righteous man should have been free from suffering—and Jesus is the only righteous man ever to walk the earth—it should have been our Lord. But He was sinless in the midst of sinful humans and their misery. Can you imagine such a thing? He lived in a world where the religious leaders hated the true God of the Bible—hated Jesus! He found but few friends, and those even denied Him in His most awful hour. He suffered misery and homelessness in this world. He suffered in every way that we might suffer, and because of that, we are to look to *"Jesus, the founder and perfecter of our faith, who for the joy that was set before him endured the cross, despising the shame, and is seated at the right hand of the throne of God"* (Hebrews 12:2). We, too, are to be motivated not by the temptations of this world, but by the joy set before us in Christ.

The Apostles echo Christ's call to suffer for Him, such as when in Romans 8:16-17 Paul says: *"The Spirit himself bears witness with our spirit that we are children of God, and if children, then heirs—heirs of God and fellow heirs with Christ, provided we suffer with him in order that we may also be glorified with him."* He goes on in verse 18 to say, *"For I consider that the sufferings of this present time are not worth comparing with the glory that is to be revealed to us."* Every believer, without exception, is called by God to suffer for Christ. Paul continues in Philippians 3:10: *"... that I may know him and the power of his resurrection, and may share his sufferings, becoming like him in his death..."* Paul encourages the church in Thessalonica with these words in 2 Thessalonians 1:4-5: *"Therefore we ourselves boast about you in the churches of God for your steadfastness and faith in all your persecutions and in the afflictions that you are enduring. This is evidence of the righteous judgment of God, that you may be considered worthy of the kingdom of God, for which you are also suffering..."*

We live in a sinful world at war with our Lord and Master, Jesus Christ. If our feet are planted on righteous paths by the living God who suffered, how can we help but suffer? First, we suffer just as the world suffers. I've spoken of my beloved brother Bill's death to cancer. Following his conversion many years ago, Bill walked the righteous paths of a Christian man. Many around him noticed the joy in which he lived his final days. *"For he [like Abraham] was looking forward to the city that has foundations, whose designer and builder is God."* (Hebrews 11:10). Bill glorified God in his life of suffering and in his death.

Amy and I have a dear friend who has suffered for years with an inherited bone disease. She rarely leaves her home, and is often in great pain when she does. Yet, she lives in utter joy because of who she is in Christ. She has every reason to complain, and yet her joy shines through her affliction. She knows her life has meaning, even in her afflictions as she serves God in prayer and supplications for others. Christians around the world suffer persecution and are ostracized because they are living for Christ. Old friends may reject us. They speak lies behind our backs. Jesus said in John 15:18: *"If the world hates you, know that it has hated me* before it hated you."

James gives us the reason for our suffering as he begins his epistle: *"Count it all joy, my brothers, when you meet trials of various kinds, for you know that the testing of your faith produces steadfastness. And let steadfastness have its full effect, that you may be perfect and complete, lacking in nothing"* (James 1:2-4). We may often hear of Christian maturity, but what is it? We spoke earlier of the goal that our heavenly Father has for each of His children. That goal is in these wonderful words of Romans 8:28-30 which I have cited before but bear repeating:

> *"And we know that for those who love God all things work together for good, for those who are called according to his purpose.* **For those whom he foreknew he also predestined to be conformed to the image of his Son**, *in order that he might be the firstborn among many brothers. And those whom he predestined he also called, and those whom he called he also justified, and those whom he justified he also glorified."*

Have you ever wanted this for your life? Do you want to be restored from the Fall and sin—from spiritual blindness and ultimate death? Do you want the joy of communion with the Savior? Then ask Him to put your feet on the eternal path of righteousness—the righteousness of our Lord Jesus Christ. It may mean that friends may desert you. It may mean that you will be persecuted and abandoned for your faithful walk. But you will find great joy, knowing that you are on the Lord's way—following Him in His righteous paths. The benefits greatly exceed the pain and difficulties. The joy far outweighs the grief.

The Path of Worship in Spirit and in Truth

Human beings are worshipers. We will either worship some one or some thing. We're like maverick electrons that must be drawn into a compound. We can't avoid it. We have been made to worship. Jesus calls us to worship Him in spirit and in truth. In John 4, we find Jesus speaking with a Samaritan woman who was drawing water from a well. During the course of their conversation, Jesus said:

> *"You worship what you do not know; we worship what we know, for salvation is from the Jews. But the hour is coming, and is now here, when the true worshipers will worship the Father in spirit and truth, for the Father is seeking such people to worship him. God is spirit, and those who worship him must worship in spirit and truth"* (John 4:22-24).

What did Jesus mean? What is it to worship God in spirit and in truth? I believe such worship consists of two central ingredients. The first ingredient is simple childlike faith—trust— in the one the Father has sent, our Lord Jesus Christ. We read in John 6:28-29: *"Then they said to him, "What must we do, to be doing the works of God?" Jesus answered them, "This is the work of God, that you believe in him whom he has sent."'* Worshiping God in spirit is to join our spirits to His eternal Spirit in trust, adoration, and obedience.

The second ingredient to worship in truth is to seek to understand and obey God's Word—our Bible. In His great high priestly prayer, Jesus prayed to the Father, *"Sanctify [believers] in the truth; your word is truth."* (John 17:17). We are to ingest God's Word so that it becomes a part of us: to memorize it and meditate upon it, and to be obedient to it. As James says in James 1:22-24: *"But be doers of the word, and not hearers only, deceiving yourselves. For if anyone is a hearer of the word and not a doer, he is like a man who looks intently at his natural face in a mirror. For he looks at himself and goes away and at once forgets what he was like."* So, we look to God's Word—His truth—to help us. Let's now look at these two parts of worship—spirit and truth—in more depth.

Worshiping God in Spirit

The writer to the Hebrews, said this in 10:25: Let's be sure we are *"...not neglecting to meet together, as is the habit of some, but encouraging one another, and all the more as you see the Day drawing near."* We Christians are called to worship God in fellowship with one another. We Americans somehow got the idea that Christianity is all about us as individuals. We erroneously may conclude that it's OK to make our faith private. But God calls us to be encouraged and strengthened as members of His Church. We are to come together for regular worship and, where appropriate, in small groups. We are to hear the Gospel of Jesus Christ with the spiritual ears that the Holy Spirit has given to us. Worshiping in spirit is to be attached to the Vine. As Jesus says in John 15:5: *"I am the vine; you are the branches. Whoever abides in me and I in him, he it is that bears much fruit, for apart from me you can do nothing."* The Good News that we are saved by grace alone through faith alone in Christ alone needs to fill our hearts and minds every day as we speak it to others and to ourselves. The Gospel isn't just for unbelievers! It is a spiritual truth that is only discerned *"in spirit."* Paul is arguing this in 1 Corinthians 2:11-16:

"For who knows a person's thoughts except the spirit of that person, which is in him? So also no one comprehends the thoughts of God except the Spirit of God. Now we have received not the spirit of the world, but the Spirit who is from God, that we might understand the things freely given us by God. And we impart this in words not taught by human wisdom but taught by the Spirit, interpreting spiritual truths to those who are spiritual. The natural person does not accept the things of the Spirit of God, for they are folly to him, and he is not able to understand them because they are spiritually discerned. The spiritual person judges all things, but is himself to be judged by no one. 'For who has understood the mind of the Lord so as to instruct him?' But we have the mind of Christ."

The Gospel of Jesus Christ isn't understood by many in the world. They have not been given the "spiritual ears" to hear and understand and believe it. In many verses in the four Gospels, Jesus says things like, *"He who has ears to hear, let him hear"* (Mark 4:9, for instance). I used to think that there were people running around back then without ears! But no, they had physical ears, but they did not have spiritual ears. The things of God's Spirit didn't make any sense to them, because the things of God's Spirit are *"spiritually discerned"* (1 Corinthians 2:14).

In community worship, we come together to speak Christ's Gospel to one another, encouraging and building up each other in our trust in the one, true God of the Bible. We sing together of God's glorious works on our behalf, and return our thanks to Him in the form of prayer. We participate in the Lord's Supper, a physical representation of the Gospel for us as we remember Christ's atoning sacrifice of His body and blood. We listen to the Word of God preached and applied to our daily lives. In doing so, we are strengthened for the week ahead. Worship is primarily for believers, not just for those attending whom we hope will receive Christ. We come into God's presence corporately, and receive the benefits of His means of grace, those things by which He has promised to nourish and encourage us. As we've noted above, the elements of worship are the preaching of the Word, prayer, praise in song, communion, and fellowship.

The Appalachian Trail runs by our former home in North Carolina. It begins in Maine and ends at Springer Mountain Georgia. It's hundreds of miles long and its paths scale mountains, cross rivers, and descend into wide valleys. I like to walk for exercise, but merely thinking about walking the length of the Appalachian Trail makes me tired. One needs strength and endurance to do it. Very few have begun at one end and marched all the way to the other end in one single trip, and even they must stop for supplies and nourishment along the way. In the same way, attempting to walk lifelong *"paths of righteousness"* without consistently feeding upon the corporate means of grace will only result in spiritual weakness and ultimate exhaustion.

Of course, we worship God every day as we pray to Him, read and study His Word, and walk with Him in justice, mercy, and humility. We have family devotions and train our children in the ways of Christ. We treat others with dignity and compassion, as the Lord has treated us. We go into our prayer closets and lay out our needs and joys before Him. All of these things are what well may be considered worship, as God commands us in Romans 12:1: *"I appeal to you therefore, brothers, by the mercies of God, to present your bodies as a living sacrifice, holy and acceptable to God,* **which is your spiritual worship**.*"* Everything we do should be an act of worship towards God. But corporate worship is central to our growth in Christ—our moving toward maturity in Him—becoming like Him in every way.

Worshiping God in Truth

Many congregations in America today hear a *"different gospel"* (Galatians 1:6-7) than that which has been once delivered to the saints. Unbelief has crept in to Christ's Church, just as it has in the centuries before us. Instead of simply believing God's truth as presented in the Bible, men and women are being told that the Bible is only one of many ways to seek God and His truth. Conformity to the world's beliefs and criticisms becomes for many a more potent source of "truth" than God's inspired Word. A materialism that denies the supernatural has taken hold of many churches, particularly in so-called "mainline" denominations. The notion of Christ being only a good example for us is taught. People still calling themselves "Christians" deny Christ's virgin birth and resurrection. A naturalistic, materialistic anti-gospel has taken the place of Christ's clear teaching that we are saved only through Christ's atoning work on the Cross.

The Bible has been received by the Church since the earliest days as inerrant and infallible in its original manuscripts and completely trustworthy. Why? Well, one reason is because the Bible teaches that it has all of these qualities. Many argue, "Well, that's just circular reasoning! The Bible says it's true, but it refers only to itself in doing so. That's a logical fallacy." While circular reasoning may be criticized when it claims to have human origins, the Bible claims to be from almighty God. Over and over in the pages of Scripture we see phrases such as *"God declares"* (Acts 2:17 for instance), and *"It is written"* (Matthew 4:4, for instance). That latter phrase refers to God's inspiration of the Old Testament and occurs 62 times in the New Testament alone. The phrase *"The word of the LORD"* is used 230 times in the Bible! Jesus prayed to the Father in John 17:17, saying, *"Sanctify them in the truth; your word is truth."* Again, our Lord said in John 10:35, *"...and the Scripture cannot be broken."* If the Lord of the universe says that Scripture is absolutely without error or fault, who can disagree? If one does disagree, it's not because of some supposed "logical fallacy." It's simply unbelief.

But the Bible isn't true only because it says so. The truth of the Holy Scriptures has been proven over and over in historical analysis. Ours is an historical faith, based in actual events proven by historical research and archaeological excavations. Prophesies of the Old Testament saints regarding the coming of the Messiah—Jesus—were fulfilled in many instances of His life on earth. In his book, *Evidence That Demands a Verdict*, (Campus Crusade for Christ, 1972), Josh

McDowell selected eight prophecies fulfilled in Jesus's life (from the sixty-one in the Old Testament) that were totally beyond human control (Pages 174-75). They were as follows: 1) Place of birth (Micah 5:2); 2) Time of birth (Daniel 9:25 & Genesis 49:10); 3) Manner of birth (Isaiah 7:14); 4) Betrayal (Psalm 41:9); 5) Manner of death (Psalm 22:16); 6) People's reactions [to His death], (Isaiah 50:6 & Psalm 109.25); 7) Piercing (Zachariah 12:10); and 8) Burial (Isaiah 53:9). McDowell goes on to say that Peter Stoner in *Science Speaks*, did some calculations to emphasize the improbability of these prophesies being fulfilled by chance:

> "...we find that the chance that any man might have lived down to the present time and fulfilled all eight prophesies is 1 in [10 to the 17th power]. That would be 1 in 100,000,000,000,000,000. In order to help us comprehend this staggering probability, Stoner illustrates it by supposing that 'we take [10 to the 17th power] silver dollars and lay them on the face of Texas. They will cover all of the state two feet deep. Now mark one of those silver dollars and stir the whole mass thoroughly, all over the state. Blindfold a man and tell him that he can travel as far as he wishes, but he must pick up one silver dollar and say this is the right one. What chance would he have of getting the right one? Just the same chance that the prophets would have had of writing these eight prophesies and having them all come true in any one man, from their day to the present time, providing they wrote them in their own wisdom.'"

The point is that these eight prophesies all came true in the life of one man—Jesus of Nazareth. The most amazing thing to me is this: If you were to show these prophesies to your unbelieving friend—their origination and fulfillment and the statistics shown by Stoner, he or she will not be moved from unbelief by them, unless he or she is supernaturally given the ability by God's Spirit. Why not? Paul answers that question in 1 Corinthians 1:18: *"For the word of the cross is folly to those who are perishing, but to us who are being saved it is the power of God."* Hasn't Paul's statement been proved over and over again in your own witnessing to people?

Furthermore, the Bible has been proven true in the lives of millions upon millions of Christian believers throughout the centuries. Many have given their lives in testimony to its divine origin. Many more have had their lives changed dramatically—brought from darkness into light—while reading its pages. Millions can testify of its truth and inerrancy as lived out in their own lives. The Bible originated in the mind of God who does not err. He cannot contradict Himself. He cannot lie. His words are always true. The Word of God is an *"anchor for the soul"* (Hebrews 6:19). We are to trust and worship the God of the Book in spirit and in truth.

One further word about the Bible. It is not only God's truth in written form, it is a book sufficient for all of our needs. It gives us meaning and purpose in the midst of an otherwise meaningless and purposeless world. To deny the Bible's truth and the fact that it supersedes all other human documents in its teaching is to be cast into darkness. The Psalmist says in Psalm 119:105, *"Your word is a lamp for my feet, a light on my path."* God's Word, like His Son, is light. All other human religion or philosophy is darkness.

One last word about worshiping in truth. Only God can define His proper worship. We must therefore look to His Word alone as our guide. Historically, this method of determining what is and what is not acceptable to God is called the "regulative principle." It includes preaching, prayer, singing hymns, psalms, and spiritual songs, participating the Lord's Supper and baptism. Most things we do, such as the time we meet, the color of the bulletin, or the order of worship are incidentals left up to each church.

The Path of Obedience

To walk in obedience to Christ is self-evident for the Christian. It's to be taken for granted that those who follow Christ will follow Him in obedience. He has laid claim on every aspect of our lives—every path that we take must be in accordance with His revealed will. He says many times in the four Gospels, things like this from John 14:15: *"If you love me, you will keep my commandments."*

Perhaps you've heard of my book, "Loving King Jesus: The Joyous Freedom of Obedience." It arose out of a businessman's Bible study that I taught for several years in San Diego. I went through my New Testament and took all of the indicatives and imperatives of Christ and the apostles and arranged them topically. Topics include: Prayer Life, Family, Business Dealings, the Church, and so on. We men studied Christ's commandments and those of His apostles every week for over a year. We talked about how this command or that command wasn't a burden to us, but freeing! Jesus said in Matthew 11:29-30: *"Take my yoke upon you, and learn from me, for I am gentle and lowly in heart, and you will find rest for your souls. For my yoke is easy, and my burden is light."* A "yoke" is a big piece of carved wood that harnesses oxen or horses together to pull a plow or a wagon. Most first century Jews saw God's law as a very burdensome yoke because they believed they needed to keep it in order to be saved. But Jesus's yoke is easy because we see His law through the eyes of His Gospel. We're saved by faith in Him, not by works, so now we love to obey Him! We love His yoke! We Christians are hitched together with Christ in love, and that makes all the difference.

God's law is the Christian's best friend. The psalmist describes the sweetness and joy of walking in paths of God's law in Psalms 119:97-104:

> *"Oh how I love your law! It is my meditation all the day. Your commandment makes me wiser than my enemies, for it is ever with me. I have more understanding than all my teachers, for your testimonies are my meditation. I understand more than the aged, for I keep your precepts. I hold back my feet from every evil way, in order to keep your word. I do not turn aside from your rules, for you have taught me. How sweet are your words to my taste, sweeter than honey to my mouth! Through your precepts I get understanding; therefore I hate every false way."*

What's not to love about God's law? The law keeps us safe from harm and evil, unjust paths. The law gives us wisdom and understanding, helping us to walk in paths that are pleasing to our heavenly Father, but also very practical and delightful. God's law is sweet as honey. To love God's law is to hate every wrongful path. To love God's law is to love Him, and to be drawn more and more into His likeness. To love God and walk in His ways is the path of joy and peace. Finally, God's law not only guides our living, but it constantly drives us back to the only true Law–Keeper in whom we hope. We don't obey perfectly because of the sin nature that still lives in us. But we have this assurance from 1 John 1:9: *"If we confess our sins, he is faithful and just to forgive us our sins and to cleanse us from all unrighteousness."* Once saved, we never can lose our relationship to God as Father, but we can lose fellowship with Him through sin. We must be careful to immediately confess sin and turn to God for His forgiveness.

The Path of Prayer

God speaks to us in His Word, and we speak to Him in our prayers. To be able to communicate our love for God to Him, our joys and our needs, as well as the needs of others, is a most wonderful benefit of being in Christ. Prayer is more than just asking God for things for yourself and others. Of course, Jesus gave us His model prayer in Matthew 6:9-13, which deals with our love, reverence for, and trust in our heavenly Father. In complete agreement with Jesus's words, someone once developed an acronym that also covers all of the bases of prayer. The acronym is ACTS, and stands for Adoration, Confession, Thanksgiving, and Supplication. You may be familiar with this model for our prayers, but it always helps to review it. It is very helpful when memorized.

"A" stands for Adoration

We bow down before God praising Him for who He is. He is all-powerful and all-wise. God sees our need before we even perceive them. His marvelous sovereignty over the events we face day-to-day comforts us. God loves each of His children with a perfect, limitless love, and grants us mercy in time of need. We simply praise God for His attributes, many of which we have highlighted in Chapter 3. Rosemary Jensen, former leader of Bible Study Fellowship and founder of Rafiki, once wrote a devotional entitled *Praying the Attributes of God*. In it, she lists thirty-one different attributes of our great God, and many Bible verses that speak to our adoring or enjoying God. It is a wonderful tool that has helped many to develop and consistently employ biblical prayer.

"C" stands for Confession and Repentance

In our church, we reserve the initial portion of our Lord's Day worship service for corporate confession of sin. Not many churches do that, I'm told. I suppose they are worried about offending a visitor. Actually, we should be more concerned with offending our heavenly Father! But confession of sin is one of the ways we worship in truth. We confess the truth about ourselves! Perhaps the most glorious benefit of being a follower of Jesus Christ, this side of eternity, is to confess sin and receive forgiveness (1 John 1:9). I suppose if someone ever took the trouble to add up the time spent in my prayer life into these four compartments of "ACTS," confession would be way ahead of the rest. Our heavenly Father wants us to confess our sins to Him. He stands ready to forgive us, restore us, and strengthen us, since in His grace, Christ's blood has covered our sins completely.

Confession must always include repentance. Repentance is not something done only once as we receive Christ and repent of our sins and of our former unbelief. Repentance always follows confession of sin. Whenever we turn to Christ, we turn away from sin. When I first came back to Christ in my mid-thirties, my family I lived in a new subdivision, and I had hooked up the cable TV without subscribing to the service. Acknowledging God's lordship over my life for the first time in my life, I confessed my sin and knew I needed to repent of my theft. So, I went to the cable company and told them that I was now a follower of Jesus Christ and confessed what I had been doing. I paid them for all the months that I had been stealing their service. To my knowledge, by God's grace, I have never again stolen anything. That's repentance. I had been turned from a lover of sin to a lover of God.

"T" stands for Thanksgiving

Paul says in 1 Thessalonians 5:18, *"...give thanks in all circumstances; for this is the will of God in Christ Jesus for you."* Thanksgiving for God's many benefits is so important, and it seems to benefit us just as much or more than it delights God. Adoration of God for His many attributes glorifies Him in our hearts and strengthens us in His service. Confession acknowledges God as holy and righteous and benefits us as we live guilt and shame-free lives. In the same manner, thanksgiving lifts our spirits and sets us free from worry, doubt, and even depression. Isaiah 61:3c is a biblical phrase that has meant so much for me over the years. When I would become depressed or unsure of God's care for me, I would remember "...*a garment of praise for a spirit of despair*" (Isaiah 61:3d, NIV). Giving God thanks in my difficulties lifted my burden and chased away the blues. Oh, God's many blessings!

Finally, "S" is for Supplication

We can easily see how we are benefited by our prayers for our own needs and for the needs of others. To maintain a record of prayers and answers to them, it's a good idea to have a prayer dairy. A friend of mine has a notebook in which he writes down his supplications to God. He draws a line down the center of each page. On the left are his prayer requests, and on the right is where he notes answers to those prayers. When he looks back after a year and sees how God has responded on behalf of himself and his family, along with others who have benefited from his supplications, he is greatly encouraged to continue praying. Prayer is God's wonderful gift that strengthens us, calms us, cheers us, stops worry, and glorifies God to the utmost. Reinhold Neibuhr said that prayer isn't just a work for Christians, it is **the** work.

Finally, we are to pray in the name of Jesus Christ. Why? Because no one can approach the throne of God immediately—without a mediator. Christ is our great High Priest who lives forever to intercede on our behalf before the Father. We cannot go to the throne of God on our own, but through His atoning work Christ represents us and is the one Mediator between God and man. Christ's "name" encompasses all of His being, His Word, and His mighty works. It means both who He is and what He has done. I have a pastor friend who always concludes his public prayers with the words, "And we pray with great confidence because we pray in the name of Jesus." Amen and Amen!

The Path of Fellowship

When we come in faith to Christ and are justified, we are ushered into a family. There's no such thing as a stand-alone Christian. Back when I was in high school, the Army football teams from West Point were some of the finest in the country. Their coach, Earl "Red" Blaik, devised an offense around a new format, focused upon what was called the "Lonesome End." The split end, Bill Carpenter, in a position we now call a wide receiver, never came back to the huddle. He stayed way out near the sidelines and ran down field as the ball was snapped. In Christianity, there are no "lonesome ends." We all join together in the huddle.

For years, I have been associated with small groups of Christian men and women, as well as a part of my church and its worship and other activities. All of the small groups have had the same purpose: to help each of its members grow in Christ through Bible study, prayer, and fellowship. Small groups are an opportunity to share life's joys and difficulties and to find spiritual help and strength in time of need. They are also a great opportunity to help others, encouraging, strengthening, and comforting one another. We need each other as we tread God's straight and right paths.

Back in the 1970s and 80s, when I was going through that time of deep trouble, I could not face it alone. A friend of mine in San Diego and I began a men's Bible study in his office in 1980 that continued for 19 years. We met in the mornings before work for an hour or so, praying for each other, encouraging one another, and studying various books of the Scriptures over the years. Looking back, although we never had more than five or six men in that study at one given time, I would estimate that over fifty different men were involved over the years. We actually had a reunion of guys who had been involved, and more than thirty attended. It was and remains one of the greatest joys of my Christian life. The emotional and prayer support I received were invaluable in getting me through the rough situations of my life during those years, as I entrusted my life to others and they entrusted their lives to me. If you aren't already, get involved in a small group.

The Path of Peace and Forgiveness

Jesus came to bring us peace. He said in John 14:27, *"Peace I leave with you; my peace I give to you. Not as the world gives do I give to you. Let not your hearts be troubled, neither let them be afraid."* In the same way, we Christians are to reflect Christ's peace in paths of honest and peaceful personal relationships. Paul commands us in Romans 12:18-19: *"If possible, so far as it depends on you, live peaceably with all. Beloved, never avenge yourselves, but leave it to the wrath of God, for it is written, 'Vengeance is mine, I will repay, says the Lord.'"*

I spoke in chapter 2 of James 4:1: *"What causes quarrels and what causes fights among you? Is it not this, that your passions are at war within you?"* The idols in our lives—inordinate affections for some created thing—cause trouble if we don't get what we want. To follow Christ is to identify these idols in our lives and turn them over to Him for destruction. In other words, we are to give up our idols for His glory and for the purpose of peace between ourselves and others. The Golden Rule is the way of peace. We are to put the needs of others on the same plane as our own needs. We are to treat others as we would like to be treated. That is the way of peace that Christ brings.

To forgive others is a necessary part of this path. Space does not allow us a full discussion of this extremely important subject. Let me merely quote these familiar words of our Lord Jesus in Matthew 6:12: *"And forgive us our debts as we also have forgiven our debtors..."* Forgiveness is not an option. We who have been forgiven much should always stand ready to forgive others. There is a real sense in which forgiveness involves a transaction. To complete the transaction, the party who gave offense recognizes his or her failure and asks the offended party for forgiveness. Then the offended party may forgive and complete the transaction. But sometimes we find that the offender won't recognize his insult or injury or the offended party doesn't want to give up his or her grudge or isn't willing to listen, and the transaction isn't completed. Nevertheless, we should always have a heart full of forgiveness, positionally ready to forgive, standing, as it were, with open arms.

I like to look at an unforgiving spirit as a heavy chain. The chain is wrapped around both the neck of the offending and the offended parties. As long as an unforgiving spirit exists the chain locks the two people together. The key belongs to the person who was hurt, the offended party. He or she has the responsibility to tell the offending party of the hurt that has been caused. Only a readiness to forgive will unlock the chain. For specific instructions on how to deal with personal conflict, read the words of our Lord in Matthew 18:15-20. We are saved, but we are still sinners and not yet glorified. Repentance of sin and forgiveness are crucial for maintaining peace in our family, local church, and community.

The Path of Service

The path of Christ is also the path of service. Jesus said to His disciples in Mark 10:42-45;

> "And Jesus called them to him and said to them, "You know that those who are considered rulers of the Gentiles lord it over them, and their great ones exercise authority over them. But it shall not be so among you. But whoever would be great among you must be your servant, and whoever would be first among you must be slave of all. For even the Son of Man came not to be served but to serve, and to give his life as a ransom for many."

To grow as a Christian is to grow in service to others. This can take many forms depending upon the gifts of the Spirit that God has given each of us. I love to teach God's Word and to write about the things of Christ. Others love to sing in the choir or to prepare food for shut-ins and for the needy. Some create art to God's glory. Others are in the home raising little ones for Christ. Still others are focused on helping in the nursery or in volunteering in their community. All of us should be consistently witnessing for Christ in our jobs, school, sports, and other community activities. There are as many ways to serve as there are Christians.

When we look at a church and try to make the decision as to whether or not to join, our question should not be, "What's in it for me?" but rather, "Where can

I make a difference in this congregation with the gifts God has given me?" Our former hometown of Asheville, North Carolina is a place noted for its reliance on the tourist industry. Even the class "A" baseball club is called the "Tourists." Likewise, we see in the American evangelical churches an emerging group who I call "ecclesiastical tourists." These are folks who wander from church to church seeking but never finding the place that can deliver to them what they want. They've got it backwards. The idea is not to be served, but to serve, as Jesus did, and gave His life as a ransom for many (Mark 10:45).

The path of serving Christ takes us into every area of our Christian lives. We don't just serve Christ on Sundays and then spend the rest of the week serving only ourselves. Christian service is a 24/7 opportunity. We'll speak more of this below when we take up the matter of Christian calling and vocation.

The Path of Stewardship

Closely related to the path of service is the path of stewardship. We are given the opportunity to worship God through the giving of tithes and offerings to His service. It has been discovered that the average Christian family in America gives something like 2% of their income to Christ's church. We have been given so much, yet we give so little. The tithe, or 10% was a standard set for the Hebrew nation back in the ancient world where most lived hand to mouth. They didn't have the great understanding of Christ and His Gospel of grace that we have today. They didn't have the great number of physical and spiritual resources that we have today. How much more than 10% should we be giving? Stewardship of our resources is a material response to God's goodness towards us. Put your feet and your family on the wonderful path of proper stewardship of that which God has given to you. It is a path of great blessing, and by as perhaps no other path, you will demonstrate to God that you fully trust Him and not your own understanding.

The Path of Justice

It would be difficult for anyone to read the Bible without seeing the theme of God's justice throughout both the Old and New Testaments. Our God is a just

God and He expects no less from His children. We may think of God's justice as His righteous judgment of sin, and we would be right in one sense. But of equal importance to our Father is His concern for justice for the poor, the downtrodden, the orphan, the widow, and the alien. These words of the psalmist speak of the arrogance of those who oppress others: *"They pour out their arrogant words; all the evildoers boast. They crush your people, O LORD, and afflict your heritage. They kill the widow and the journer, and murder the fatherless..."* (Psalm 94:4-6). But the LORD does see—the God of Jacob does take notice! He says in Isaiah 10:1-2: *"Woe to those who decree iniquitous decrees, and the writers who keep writing oppression, to turn aside the needy from justice and to rob the poor of my people of their right, that widows may be their spoil, and that they may make the fatherless their prey!"*

The Christian path of justice seeks to alleviate suffering, oppression, poverty, and disease among those who live in difficult circumstances. Justice seeks the best for one's neighbor. This requires sacrifice on our part. James 1:27 says that justice is at the very center of true religion: *"Religion that is pure and undefiled before God, the Father, is this: to visit orphans and widows in their affliction, and to keep oneself unstained from the world."* Finally, we read these words from the prophet Micah in 6:8: *"He has told you, O man, what is good; and what does the LORD require of you but to do justice, and to love kindness, and to walk humbly with your God?"*

The Path of Vocation

During the middle ages, the church pushed a false dichotomy between the secular and sacred callings in life. Those who entered monasteries or nunneries, following the call of service to the church as priests or nuns, were deemed to be in sacred callings. Other folks like farmers and bricklayers and carpenters and blacksmiths were said to be engaged in secular activities. The Reformation brought back into Christ's Church the truth that all callings are sacred.

Christians are called to Christ from a culture formed by people generally hostile to or indifferent to Christianity. Jesus says of us in Matthew 5:13 and 14: *"You are the salt of the earth."* and *"You are the light of the world."* We are to be salt and light. Salt was used with some of the ancient Hebrew sacrifices to remind them of God's covenant with His people. Salt is also a preservative that was used extensively in the ancient world. Today, salt is used to flavor food. Light, of course, is that which gives us the ability to see with our eyes. By these terms, Jesus is telling us that we are to influence for good the culture in which we find ourselves. This is a sacred calling and it is to be accomplished by businessmen, mothers, physicians, carpenters, teachers, firemen, and every other calling in which we find ourselves, including pastors. We are to preserve the good, remembering God's covenant in Christ, and shed light on the evil. In so doing we seek to be a blessing to the culture in which we live. Every Christian is called to this sacred task.

The Path of Evangelism

When I was a new Christian some 40 years ago, I attended Scott Memorial Baptist church in San Diego's North Park where Tim LaHaye was the pastor. I remember going out one day to witness to people in the local community. We were given small tracts that talked about the five keys to God's kingdom, declaring how a person could be saved. On the rear of the tract was a word to Christians that I still remember. It said, "Witnessing is sharing Christ in the power of the Holy Spirit and leaving the results to God." As I've grown in Christ, that still sticks with me. We are to be "sowers" of the seed of God's Word. It is God who gives the increase, or growth (1 Corinthians 3:7). It is God who saves, not us. That is a very comforting and encouraging fact. We merely participate in God's plan; we aren't responsible for lost sinners. This understanding is not a call to inactivity. It should free us to plant God's Gospel truth in many hearts and lives. We know God has loved ones out there. It's just that they don't know it yet and we don't know who they are.

In the Great Commission of Matthew 28:18-20, Jesus says this:

> ***"All authority in heaven and on earth has been given to me.*** *Go therefore and make disciples of all nations, baptizing them in the name of the Father and of the Son and of the Holy Spirit, teaching them to observe all that I have commanded you. And behold, I am with you always, to the end of the age."*

"All authority" truly means *all* authority. We witness about God's saving grace knowing that the One about whom we witness has all authority and power. But Jesus calls each of us to sow the seed of the gospel. This activity is for all Christians, not just some, like pastors and elders or people who feel comfortable sharing their faith. In 1 Peter 3:15, Peter says, *"...but in your hearts honor Christ the Lord as holy, always being prepared to make a defense to anyone who asks you for a reason for the hope that is in you; yet do it with gentleness and respect."* Be prepared. Think about what Christ has done for you. Be ready to share a favorite verse. Remember that *"...the word of God is living and active, sharper than any two-edged sword, piercing to the division of soul and of spirit, of joints and of marrow, and discerning the thoughts and intentions of the heart."* (Hebrews 4:12). The Gospel either softens hearts or hardens hearts. We need to remember that it is God who brings people to salvation. We are merely carrying the message to a lost and dying world.

In the mountains east of San Diego, out toward the desert of the Imperial Valley, you will see some gigantic boulders. Some seem to be as big as a small house. They are smooth and rounded and for years when old highway 80 was in service, they served as billboards for religious groups and others to proclaim their message. By far the most frequent message was relayed in two simple words: "Jesus Saves." I used to think how odd that message was. But it is simply the gospel in two words. Jesus does indeed save (Luke 19:10). We merely spread the word of His great and free salvation.

The Path of Joy

Any discussion of Christ–centered paths must conclude with the path of joy. In every corner of the world all people are seeking to be happy. What's the difference between joy and happiness? Simply put, happiness is the result of pleasant and agreeable circumstances. Christian joy is not dependent upon circumstances. Christian joy comes in the deep–seated, foundational understanding that all is well, regardless of our circumstances. Back in the late 1800s, a Christian by the name of Horatio Spafford lost his daughters when their ship suddenly sank in the middle of the Atlantic Ocean. His wife sent him a telegram which said, "Saved alone." Horribly saddened by their loss, Horatio nevertheless penned these words of true joy in the midst of terrible sadness:

> "When peace like a river attendeth my soul,
> When sorrows like sea billows roll,
> Whatever my lot, thou hast taught me to say,
> It is well, it is well, with my soul.
>
> "Though Satan may buffet, though trials may come,
> Let this blest assurance control,
> That Christ has regarded my helpless estate,
> And has shed His own blood for my soul.
>
> "My sin—O the bliss of this glorious thought—
> My sin, not in part, but in whole,
> Is nailed to the cross and I bear it no more,
> Praise the Lord, praise the Lord, O my soul.
>
> O Lord haste the day when my faith shall be sight,
> The clouds be rolled back like a scroll,
> The trumpet shall sound, and the Lord shall descend,
> Even so—it is well with my soul."

Christian joy is centered in God's *shalom*—His peace that passes all understanding (Philippians 4:7). Though sickness, sadness, and trouble of all kinds may come, our feet are firmly planted on the hope that God has put within each of us. *"We have this as a sure and steadfast anchor of the soul, a hope that enters into the inner place behind the curtain, where Jesus has gone as a forerunner on our behalf..."* (Hebrews 6:19–20).

Conclusion

One of my favorite verses is Ephesians 2:10: *"For we are his workmanship, created in Christ Jesus for good works, which God prepared beforehand, that we should walk in them."* The dignity and eternal purpose that our Father has bestowed upon each of His children is breathtaking. By His grace alone, God has lifted each of us up from a desolate, dead-end, meaningless existence and made us partners in His plan for the ages. Sometimes, when I feel down and lose my sense of direction, I ponder that verse. By His mighty power and grace, God has take our feet off of the paths of defeat and death and placed them on paths of victory and life. What you and I do today counts forever.

One day we will all look back and see how God worked out the counsel of His sovereign will through us. We will see each of the threads of our lives that God has woven into the great tapestry of redemptive history. Ultimately, we will all leave the various paths of this life. But new, even more wonderful paths await us as we continue to serve Christ on a new and redeemed heavens and earth. In that glorious day, unburdened by the sin that now so easily besets us, we will truly glorify God and enjoy Him forever.

Questions for Further Study

These verses each speak of one of the paths to which each Christian is called. Write in the appropriate path next to each verse:

1. Hebrews 11:6 ....

2. Romans 5:18 ....

3. Psalm 103:17-18 ....

4. Hebrews 10:25 ....

5. 1 Timothy 2:8 ....

6. Psalm 96:9 ....

7. Galatians 5:13 ....

8. Proverbs 29:7 ....

9. Matthew 18:21-22 ....

10. John 15:11 ....

Afterword

A friend of mine was witnessing to a young man about Christ. The youth sneered and said, "Well, that's all 'pie-in-the-sky-by-and-by' stuff. You have to die to see if it's really true." How wrong the young man was! We who have trusted Christ for salvation have eternal life **now**. We have assurance of our new birth and adoption as sons of God. We have assurance of His perfect, unconditional love for us. We have God's Word on it! And we have the down payment of God's Spirit living within us. We have a **certain** hope of spending eternity with Christ, our Lord and Savior. The Gospel is for right now! What could possibly be better than that?

In the Beatitudes of our Lord's Sermon on the Mount, (Matthew 5:3-11), He describes the man or woman who has been saved by grace alone. What we do naturally flows out of who we are. We are "*new creations*" (2 Corinthians 5:17). As new creatures in Christ, we are to be different from all other people. We are blessed in so many ways, not because of what we have done to deserve it, which is nothing, but because of what Christ has done to accomplish it for us. The God who created the universe has brought each one of us into a loving and close relationship to Himself as members of His Church—His family. We are poor in spirit, mournful, meek, hungering and thirsting after righteousness, merciful, pure in heart, peacemakers, and even persecuted—yet blessed. We are blessed even in attitudes and situations that the world finds distasteful, even abhorrent. Why? Because of the certain knowledge that in Christ, God is on our side. He is our God and we are His people.

We therefore walk as Jesus walked, on paths of humility and righteousness. Jesus, who has all authority in heaven and on earth, walks by our side. He says to each of us, "*Never will I leave you, never will I forsake you*" (Hebrews 13:5). What other "god" offers this assurance? What other god has this authority and power? What other god loves you in spite of who you were—sinful, godless, and an enemy? What other god would go willingly to a Roman cross for you? None other than Jesus Christ. Regardless of where our Lord leads us, we can be content, joyful, and secure in the certain knowledge that His promises are true. His power is unassailable. His love for His brothers and sisters is beyond the stars in its height and depth and breadth.

So we come back to these words: *"Trust in the LORD with all your heart, and do not lean on your own understanding. In all your ways acknowledge him, and he will make straight your paths."* Twenty-nine words that contain the wisdom of God for all believers. We trust only God for salvation and for our every need. We reject our own sinful understanding and worldview. Rather, we rely only upon God's wisdom, power, mercy, and grace each day as to how we can each work for good within the world's system. In every way in which we walk, we acknowledge God for who He is, and trust Him to put our feet on righteous paths—paths that seek His glory and our eternal joy. In the words of Paul in 1 Corinthians 10:31, *"So, whether you eat or drink, or whatever you do, do all to the glory of God."*

May God richly bless you with great joy and peace as you grow in the knowledge and wisdom of God, walking in the One who loves you and gave Himself for you.

Abbreviated Bibliography

General References

Berhof, Louis. *Systematic Theology*. Grand Rapids, MI: Eerdmans, 1996.

Elwell, Walter A., Editor. *Evangelical Dictionary of Theology*. Grand Rapids, MI: Baker Academic, 2001.

Frame, John M. *The Doctrine of the Christian Life*. Phillipsburg, NJ: P&R Publishing, 2008.

Grudem, Wayne. *Systematic Theology: An Introduction to Biblical Doctrine*. Grand Rapids, MI: Zondervan, 1994.

Chapter 1: Trust in the LORD with All of Your Heart

Beasley, Robert C., *The Commandments of Christ*, Phillipsburg, NJ: P&R Publishing, 1999.

Boice, James Montgomery. *Standing on the Rock: Upholding Biblical Authority in a Secular Age*. Grand Rapids, MI: Kregel, 1998.

Bridges, Jerry. *Is God Really in Control? Trusting God in a World of Hurt*. Colorado Springs, CO: Navpress, 2006.

Bridges, Jerry. *Trusting God: Even When Life Hurts*. Colorado Springs, CO: Navpress, 1988.

White, James R. *Scripture Alone*. Bloomington, MN: Bethany House, 2004.

Chapter 2: And Lean Not on Your Own Understanding

Anderson, Neil T., et al. *Breaking the Bondage of Legalism*. Eugene OR: Harvest House, 2003.

Beale, G. K. *We Become What We Worship: A Biblical Theology of Idolatry*. Downers Grove, IL: IVP Academic, 2008.

Bridges, Jerry. *Respectable Sins: Confronting the Sins We Tolerate*. Colorado Springs, CO: Navpress, 2007.

Downey, Patrick. *Desperately Wicked: Philosophy, Christianity, and the Human Heart*. Madison, WI: InterVarsity, 2009.

Fitzpatrick, Elyse. *Idols of the Heart: Learning to Long for God Alone*. Phillipsburg, NJ: P&R Publishing, 2001.

Horton, Michael. *Christless Christianity*. Grand Rapids, MI: Baker Books, 2008.

Keller, Timothy. *Counterfeit Gods: The Empty Promises of Money, Sex, and Power, and the Only Hope that Matters*. New York, NY: Dutton, 2009.

Machen, J. Gresham. *The Christian View of Man*. Carlisle, PA: Banner of Truth, 2002.

Minter, Kelly. *No Other Gods: Confronting Our Modern Day Idols*. Colorado Springs, CO: David C. Cook, 2008.

Plantinga, Cornelius, Jr. *Not the Way It's Supposed to Be: A Breviary of Sin*. Grand Rapids, MI: Eerdmans, 1995.

Schlossberg, Herbert. *Idols for Destruction: The Conflict of Christian Faith and American Culture*. Wheaton, IL: Crossway, 1990.

Shuster, Marguerite. *The Fall and Sin*. Grand Rapids, MI: Eerdmans, 2004.

Stedman, Ray C. *Understanding Man*. Waco, TX: Word Books, 1971

Chapter 3: In All Your Ways Acknowledge Him

Bridges, Jerry. *Transforming Grace: Living Confidently in God's Unfailing Love*. Colorado Springs, CO: Navpress, 1991.

Frame, John M. *The Doctrine of the Knowledge of God*. Phillipsburg, NJ: P&R Publishing, 1987.

Jensen, Rosemary. *Praying the Attributes of God*. Grand Rapids, MI: Kregel, 2002.

Packer, J. I. *Knowing God*. Downers Grove, IL: InterVarsity, 1973.

Pink, Arthur W. *Gleanings in the Godhead*. Chicago, IL: Moody, 1975.

Sproul, R.C. *The Invisible Hand: Do All Things Really Work for Good?* Dallas, TX: Word, 1996.

Chapter 4: And He Will Direct Your Paths

Frame, John M. *Worship in Spirit and Truth*. Phillipsburg, NJ: P&R Publishing, 1996.

Keller, Timothy. *Generous Justice: How God's Grace Makes Us Just*. New York, NY: Penguin, 2010.

Mack, Wayne A. et al. *Humility: The Forgotten Virtue*. Phillipsburg, NJ: P&R Publishing, 2005.

McDowell, Josh. *Evidence That Demands a Verdict*. Campus Crusade for Christ, 1972.

Packer, J.I. *Growing in Christ*. Wheaton, IL: Crossway, 1994.

Pink, Arthur W. *The Life of Faith: What Has God Done for You?* Fearn, Rosshire, Scotland: Christian Focus, 2003.

Pratt, Richard L. Jr. *Pray With Your Eyes Open*. Phillipsburg, NJ: P&R Publishing, 1987.

Trinity Hymnal, Atlanta, GA: Great Commission Publications, 1991.

Appendix: Verses About Total Depravity or Total Inability

The following are verses which teach the doctrine of total depravity and salvation by God's grace alone--that regeneration or the new birth logically precedes faith in Christ. My goal in sharing them is simply to help us understand what the Bible teaches about who we are and why God Himself had to submit Himself to the Cross in order to save us from our sin and enmity against Him. Prayerfully let them all flow over you, asking God to give you understanding. The first verse speaks of how we got to be the way we are:

Genesis 2:16-17: *"And the LORD God commanded the man, "You are free to eat from any tree in the garden; but you must not eat from the tree of the knowledge of good and evil, for when you eat of it you will surely die."*

1. The death God meant was not immediate physical death, but complete alienation from Himself, or spiritual death. Subsequently, Adam's death passed to all men everywhere.

Romans 5:12: *"Therefore, just as sin entered the world through one man, and death through sin, and in this way death came to all men, because all sinned..."*

Ephesians 2:1-3: *"As for you, you were dead in your transgressions and sins, in which you used to live when you followed the ways of this world and of the ruler of the kingdom of the air, the spirit who is now at work in those who are disobedient. All of us also lived among them at one time, gratifying the cravings of our sinful nature and following its desires and thoughts. Like the rest, we were by nature objects of wrath."*

Colossians 2:13: *"When you were dead in your sins and in the uncircumcision of your sinful nature, God made you alive with Christ..."*

2. In the Psalms, David also confessed that he was born in sin:

Psalms 51:5: *"Surely I was sinful at birth, sinful from the time my mother conceived me."*

Psalms 58:3: *"Even from birth the wicked go astray; from the womb they are wayward and speak lies."*

3. Because of spiritual death, Jesus taught that we must be regenerated to enter God's kingdom:

John 3:5-7: "*Jesus answered, "I tell you the truth, no one can enter the kingdom of God unless he is born of water and the Spirit. Flesh gives birth to flesh, but the Spirit gives birth to spirit. You should not be surprised at my saying, 'You must be born again.'"*

John 1:12-13: "*Yet to all who received him, to those who believed in his name, he gave the right to become children of God—children born not of natural descent, nor of human decision or a husband's will, but born of God.*"

4. Immediately following the Fall, sin cast its death-spell upon all men:

Genesis 6:5: "*The LORD saw how great man's wickedness on the earth had become, and that every inclination of the thoughts of his heart was only evil all the time.*" (The natural man was and is "*non posse non peccare*"--not able not to sin).

Titus 3:3: "*At one time we too were foolish, disobedient, deceived and enslaved by all kinds of passions and pleasures. We lived in malice and envy, being hated and hating one another.*"

5. The curse of sin still rests upon all people:

Job 15:14-16: "*What is man, that he could be pure, or one born of woman, that he could be righteous? If God places no trust in his holy ones, if even the heavens are not pure in his eyes, how much less man, who is vile and corrupt, who drinks up evil like water!*"

Psalms 130:3: "*If you, O LORD, kept a record of sins, O Lord, who could stand?*"

Psalms 143:2: "*Do not bring your servant into judgment, for no one living is righteous before you.*"

Proverbs 20:9: "*Who can say, "I have kept my heart pure; I am clean and without sin"?*"

Ecclesiastes 7:20: "*There is not a righteous man on earth who does what is right and never sins.*"

Ecclesiastes 7:29: *"This only have I found: God made mankind upright, but men have gone in search of many schemes."*

Isaiah 53:6: *"We all, like sheep, have gone astray, each of us has turned to his own way..."*

Isaiah 64:6: *"All of us have become like one who is unclean, and all our righteous acts are like filthy rags; we all shrivel up like a leaf, and like the wind our sins sweep us away."*

Romans 3:9-12: *"What shall we conclude then? Are we any better? Not at all! We have already made the charge that Jews and Gentiles alike are all under sin. As it is written: "There is no one righteous, not even one; there is no one who understands, no one who seeks God. All have turned away, they have together become worthless; there is no one who does good, not even one."*

James 3:5-6: *"Likewise the tongue is a small part of the body, but it makes great boasts. Consider what a great forest is set on fire by a small spark. The tongue also is a fire, a world of evil among the parts of the body. It corrupts the whole person, sets the whole course of his life on fire, and is itself set on fire by hell."*

1 John 1:8: *"If we claim to be without sin, we deceive ourselves and the truth is not in us."*

6. Not only are we all sinners, sin that affects the whole person, so that we cannot do any good thing, neither can we change, or go from *non posse non peccare* to *posse peccare—posse non peccare*. (From "Not possible not to sin" to "Possible to sin—possible not to sin.")

Job 14:4: *"Who can bring what is pure from the impure? No one!"*

Jeremiah 13:23: *"Can the Ethiopian change his skin or the leopard its spots? Neither can you do good who are accustomed to doing evil."*

Matthew 7:16-18: *"By their fruit you will recognize them. Do people pick grapes from thorn bushes, or figs from thistles? Likewise every good tree bears good fruit, but a bad tree bears bad fruit. A good tree cannot bear bad fruit, and a bad tree cannot bear good fruit."*

Matthew 12:33: *"Make a tree good and its fruit will be good, or make a tree bad and its fruit will be bad, for a tree is recognized by its fruit."*

Made in the USA
Columbia, SC
06 September 2024